The Transforming Image

JEAN HALL

The Transforming Image: A Study of Shelley's Major Poetry

UNIVERSITY OF ILLINOIS PRESS

Urbana Chicago London

To My Parents
Raymond and Dorothy Rogers

LIBRARY OF CONGRESS CATALOGING IN PUBLICATION DATA

Hall, Jean, 1941–
    The transforming image.

    Includes bibliographical references and index.
    1. Shelley, Percy Bysshe, 1792–1822—Criticism and
interpretation.   I. Title.
PR5438.H34   821'.7   80-12748
ISBN 0-252-00766-2

Contents

Acknowledgments

I thank W. T. Jones, Brian Wilkie, Robert F. Gleckner, Harold Bloom, John W. Wright, Carol Collins, Margaret Dana, and Carol Daeley, who all read the manuscript at one stage or another and offered helpful suggestions.

The Transforming Image

Introduction

Because of his enthusiasm for Plato, many of Shelley's readers have viewed him as a Platonist, or at least as some species of transcendentalist.[1] This has been so since the beginning of his fame. However, Shelley also read extensively in the literature of British Empiricism. In 1954 C. E. Pulos effectively analyzed Shelley's assimilation of the Empirical heritage, concluding that he is a philosophical skeptic who "does not make dogmatical assertions about unknowable things but expresses tentative feelings about things recognized as unknowable."[2] The difference between Platonic transcendentalism and Empirical skepticism obviously is immense, and naturally, suggests two incompatible visions of Shelley's poetry.[3] My reading of Shelley originates in a recognition of this difficulty, which seems to me the crucial problem in Shelley studies.

One way of dealing with Shelley's apparent philosophical inconsistency is to suggest that on some deeper level, his Platonism

integrates with his Empiricism. This has been the thrust of Earl
R. Wasserman's very ambitious contemporary reading of Shelley.[4]
He has reconstructed Shelley's Empiricism to yield an epistemol-
ogy that delivers transcendentalist results. Although Wasserman
begins by describing the Shelleyan primal world unity as "a
nontheistic and nontranscendent Absolute,"[5] still, the poet's philosophy emphasizes "distinctions between appearance and reality,
diversity and unity, thing and idea,"[6] and "allows . . . indisputably present phenomena to serve as means of an imaginative
leap from the realm of Existence into the realm of Being on which
it depends."[7] Wasserman's Shelley lives amidst the empirical
veils of appearance and mutability, which from time to time part
by the aegis of imaginative inspiration to reveal an unchanging
real Absolute. From his Empirical beginnings this Shelley has
arrived at what looks like an unavoidably transcendental conclusion.[8]

But John W. Wright has offered an Empirical approach to
Shelley which sidesteps this sort of transcendentalism.[9] Wright
sees the poet's speculations as essentially directed toward a philosophy of experience rather than, as Wasserman assumes, a
transcendental ontology. In Wright's discussion, Wasserman's absolute "Being" is converted into the poet's sense of being in the
world, and unity becomes not the result of a "leap from the realm
of Existence into the realm of Being" but an act of mind: "the
mind is that unity which it creates among the myriad relations and
distinctions it apprehends. Metaphor therefore is more an act of
transcendence than a manifestation of a transcendent reality."[10]
Hence, the relations of life no longer are determined by Wasserman's dualistic divisions "between appearance and reality, diversity and unity, thing and idea"—they simply are a texture of
being, a sense of one thing changing into another. Shelley pos-
sesses not Reality but his feeling for experience, and his world
becomes "a mind-made poem in which metaphor is tantamount
to metamorphosis and imagination is the agent of transfiguration

in human nature."[11] Thus, Wright repudiates a Platonic reading of Shelley, a position shared by Harold Bloom, the most distinguished of Shelley's modern critics to take that view.[12]

Although my study begins in sympathy with Wright's analysis, for reasons that will become clear in the first chapter I have chosen to stress Shelley's imagery rather than his metaphor: Wright's central idea of the metamorphosis of metaphor becomes for me transformation of imagery. Both of us feel that Shelley lives in a world of appearance (metaphor, images) and its transformation; and that the thrust of his poetry is not to reach the realm of a real Absolute, but to enact the transformation of forms. From this perspective, Pulos seems correct about Shelley's skepticism. Shelley denies the possibility of knowing Reality, and builds his poetry on what we can know—our constantly changing sense of existence.

This book traces the poet's developing treatment of transformation through a mainly chronological reading of the major poetry, beginning with *Alastor* (1815), which implies Shelley's need to commit himself to the transformations of appearance, and the "Hymn to Intellectual Beauty" (1816), which first exhibits Shelley's ability to create poetic transformations. Next, "Mont Blanc" (1816) and "Ode to the West Wind" (1820) show Shelley contending with nature to transform it into a humanly significant form. *Prometheus Unbound* exaggerates this transformation of nature until it becomes a transformation of the entire world, the continuous creation of a poetic universe by means of ecstatic lyricism. And in the final major poetry (*Epipsychidion*, 1821; *Adonais*, 1821; *The Triumph of Life*, 1822) the radical implications of Shelley's procedure flower: these are lyrics built upon a constantly transforming world of appearance, existing only through their incessant movement which wings not through to a transcendental Absolute but into a self-created heaven of the moment, living in the poet's song and dying as the melody fades away, which eventually it must.

NOTES

1. The notable modern treatment is James A. Notopoulos, *The Platonism of Shelley* (Durham, N.C., 1949). For a selection of Platonically influenced criticism on Shelley, see Carlos Baker, *Shelley's Major Poetry: The Fabric of a Vision* (New York, 1948, 1961); Milton Wilson, *Shelley's Later Poetry: A Study of His Prophetic Imagination* (New York, 1959); Neville Rogers, *Shelley at Work: A Critical Inquiry* (Oxford, 1956); and Ross Greig Woodman, *The Apocalyptic Vision in the Poetry of Shelley*, University of Toronto Department of English Studies and Texts, no. 12 (Toronto, 1964).

2. C. E. Pulos, *The Deep Truth: A Study of Shelley's Scepticism* (Lincoln, Neb., 1954, 1962), p. 77.

3. See M. H. Abrams, "Shelley and Romantic Platonism," in *The Mirror and the Lamp: Romantic Theory and the Critical Tradition* (New York, 1953), pp. 126–31. "In the 'Defence' [Plato and "the English sensational psychologists"] remain imperfectly assimilated, so that one can discriminate two planes of thought in Shelley's aesthetics—one Platonistic and mimetic, the other psychological and expressive—applied alternately, as it were, to each of the major topics under discussion. The combination effected a loosely articulated critical theory . . ." (pp. 126–27).

4. Earl R. Wasserman, *Shelley: A Critical Reading* (Baltimore, 1971). Earlier versions of this material appeared in the following: *The Subtler Language: Critical Readings of Neoclassic and Romantic Poems* (Baltimore, 1959); *Shelley's Prometheus Unbound: A Critical Study* (Baltimore, 1965); and "Shelley's Last Poetics: A Reconsideration," in *From Sensibility to Romanticism: Essays Presented to Frederick A. Pottle*, ed. F. W. Hilles and Harold Bloom (New Haven, 1965). All future citations of Wasserman will refer to *Shelley: A Critical Reading*.

5. Wasserman, *Shelley*, p. 147.

6. Ibid.

7. Ibid., p. 153.

8. Although I disagree with Wasserman's philosophical analysis, I would not want to deny that he has given some of Shelley's poetry perhaps the best reading it has received. Wasserman's readings have influenced me, even when I have differed from them.

9. John W. Wright, *Shelley's Myth of Metaphor* (Athens, Ga., 1970).

10. Ibid., p. 44.

11. Ibid., p. 25.

12. Harold Bloom, *Shelley's Mythmaking* (New Haven, Conn., 1959); "Percy Bysshe Shelley" in *The Visionary Company: A Reading of English Romantic Poetry*, revised and enlarged edition (Ithaca, N.Y., 1971); and "The Unpastured Sea: An Introduction to Shelley" in *The Ringers in the*

Tower: Studies in Romantic Tradition (Chicago and London, 1971). One of
the most vigorous statements of Bloom's position is to be found on pp.
94–95 of *The Ringers in the Tower*: "The fatal aesthetic error, in reading
Prometheus Unbound or any other substantial work by Shelley, is to start
with the assumption that one is about to read Platonic poetry. . . .
Shelley's skeptical and provisional idealism is *not* Plato's, and Shelley's
major poems are mythopoeic, and not translatable into any terms but
their own highly original ones. . . . Nothing is further from Shelley's
mind and art than the Platonic view of knowledge, and nothing is further
from Shelley's tentative myths than the dogmatic myths of Plato. It is
one of the genuine oddities of critical history that a tough-minded Humean poet, though plagued also by an idealistic and pseudo-Platonic heart,
should have acquired the reputation of having sought beauty or truth in
any Platonic way or sense whatsoever."

CHAPTER ONE

The Poetics of Transformation

Before tracing Shelley's relationship to the Empirical philosophers and making it clear how their conclusions helped him
abandon the notion of transcendental Absolutes, it will be necessary to briefly sketch the history of British Empiricism. The
century-long development of Empiricism is itself pointed toward
the rejection of a realist ontology; by the early nineteenth century many sensitive readers of the Empirical canon could have
come to conclusions similar to Shelley's.

Ironically, the first authoritative formulation of the Empirical
approach, by Locke, was intended to rigorously certify an empirical realism. That is, Locke hoped to make clear the relationship
of man's mind to an indisputably existing external reality conveyed to us by the report of our senses. For Locke, in order to
clarify our knowledge we must reduce it to its sensory origins,
and then carefully audit combinations of our ideas, from simple to
complex, so that no vacuities or inaccuracies creep in. The com-

pleted edifice of Lockean knowledge has two properties: 1) its raw
material is the flow of our sensory experience, which presents
itself in a serial fashion—one sensation comes, then another, then
another, and so forth; 2) unities are constructed from this raw
material by an additive process, which also is serial—one idea
relates to another, which relates to another, then another, and so
on.

Locke was comfortable with such a procedure because he had a
strong commonsense belief in an external reality that caused our
sense impressions. The Lockean mind is a kind of computer
which adds up serially presented impressions caused by real
things; and unless a person is deranged, it will be clear to him
when a sum total of impressions adds up to a real object. For
instance, the impressions "red," "sweet," "spherical" will come,
and the subject then will realize that they add up to the unity
"apple," rather than continuing his sensory computation to other
contiguous impressions such as, perhaps, "blue," "drizzly,"
"moist," which are not part of "apple," although they may be
part of the ongoing sensory flow. But as W. T. Jones remarks,
". . . do we . . . compound 'red,' 'sweet,' 'spherical,' and so
forth together to make the idea of apple? Or do we see an apple
and then, by a process of selective attention, note that it is red,
spherical, and so on? Surely, the latter. The world of ordinary
experience is a world of objects, and Locke's simple ideas, so far
from being starting points of experience, are terminal points." [1]

Thus, the Lockean account of experience presents the problem
of objective unities—of how we recognize them, and what they
are. This soon became evident to philosophers of the Empirical
school. They pointed out that what Lockean man is aware of is
"sense impressions" and "ideas," not objective "things." Unfortunately, "red" plus "sweet" plus "spherical" is not really equal to
"apple," and the external world that Locke confidently assumed
we were perceiving suddenly is cut loose from our impressions,
which now exist in a kind of phenomenological vacuum. All

Locke really can say is that we do have impressions, and that they
do come in a flow which seems to present leitmotifs (the series
"red," "sweet," "spherical" periodically recurs, for example)—
but why this happens, and what the process means, is unclear.
Instead of totaling up, Lockean experience continues aggregating
forever, with no clear boundaries between parts of the flow, and
no definitive summation in sight.

   Given this situation, Berkeley invoked the Author of Nature to
organize our impressions into unities which signify. For Berkeley, an elaborate theistic idealism, in which God certifies the objectivity of our experience, becomes the only way of regaining the
real world of apples and drizzly rains that Locke thought obviously was there. But Hume cannot accept this Berkeleyan
organization, for it assumes a grand objective unity—God—for
which he sees no evidence in his own phenomenological experience. Impressions do occur in series for Hume; but those series do
not necessarily signify. Even we ourselves fail to signify, for we
experience our own unity or personal identity as a phenomenological flow, just as we experience everything else. Therefore,
when Hume tries to "enter most intimately into what I call
myself," he can experience himself only as "a bundle or collection
of different perceptions, which succeed each other with an inconceivable rapidity, and are in perpetual flux and movement."[2] The
Humean world is a congeries of loose "collections" and "bun-
dles": in everything, there is no rational connection of cause and
effect uniting our flow of impressions. When examined, the
smooth river of our experience reveals itself as a series of jerks and
starts, isolated impressions that do not necessarily connect with
what comes before and what comes after. The element that creates
our sense of flow is habit—our irrational expectation that impressions will come again in the same series that they came before.
With Hume, British Empiricism turns skeptical, affirms only
that we have experience, but denies that we can discover reliably
what that experience is experience of. Knowledge becomes an

affair of probability, but even that probability is shaky because it involves only irrational expectations grounded on habit—not on real evidence.

This Humean form of British Empiricism was Shelley's legacy, both through the original work of Hume and in the adaptations of William Godwin and William Drummond.[3] Almost from the first, it is clear that the inability to construct an ontology struck Shelley as an exhilarating freedom. In the early essay *On Life* (circa 1812–14) Shelley coins an Empirical phrase which is to become thematic in his prose: triumphantly he announces that "nothing exists but as it is perceived," revealing himself to have accepted the Empirical world of strictly phenomenological experience. This view, "though startling to the apprehension, is, in fact, that which the habitual sense of [life's] repeated combinations has extinguished in us. It strips, as it were, the painted curtain from this scene of things."[4] The notion of experience as simply a phenomenal flow is welcome to Shelley because it suggests that our "habitual sense of . . . repeated combinations" is only one of the possible orders of experience, and that it can be swept away to admit novelty. He praises the newness of childhood vision, when "We less habitually distinguished all that we saw and felt, from ourselves. They seemed as it were to constitute one mass." In the adult, such states are less frequent, and "precede, or accompany, or follow an unusually intense and vivid apprehension of life" (VI, 195–96). These remarks anticipate the kernel of Shelley's artistic program: to dissolve our habitually serial sense of life through brief, fusive experiences that for a time can transform our entire outlook.

As an enthusiastic and intuitional poet, Shelley has sensed a way of achieving unity that had not occurred to the Empirical philosophers and would not have appealed to them even if it had. His sense of unity comes from moments of fusive intuition, fleeting ecstasies in which the world suddenly is sensed as a whole. As he says in *A Defence of Poetry*, the inspired poet "participates in the eternal, the infinite, and the one; as far as relates to his conceptions, time and place and number are not" (VII, 112).

Of course, such language makes Shelley begin to sound less like an Empiricist than a Platonist. But it wasn't Plato's theory of Forms that engaged him; it was Plato's language and imagery. As he says in the *Defence*, "Plato was essentially a poet—the truth and splendour of his imagery, and the melody of his language, is the most intense that it is possible to conceive" (VII, 114); and in the Preface to his translation of the *Symposium*, Shelley remarks that Plato's "excellence consists especially in intuition" (VII, 162). It seems to me that Shelley's combination of Empiricism and Platonism is not intended to be a philosophical theory but a program for poetry. He accepts the Empirical description of our experience as a phenomenal flow, but then he goes to Plato for the idea that the flow can be significantly organized through moments of poetic intuition.

This program does not necessarily imply the intuitional revelation of a Platonic world of objective Existence; instead, it may suggest that unity could be not an "object" or "thing" but a quality of experience—an unusually vivid and organized state of being. To see something of what I mean, consider the well-known figure on the following page.[5] Some people see two facing profiles in this figure, but others see a vase. Whichever form one sees, it does not emerge gradually but in a flash of revelation that instantly structures the entire field of perception. This mode of understanding is neither serial nor aggregative. Instead of a Lockean flow of data that adds up to something, here we have a single datum that can be construed in more than one way, by a transformation of the interpretive context. If the viewer places the white area of the figure as the background and the black area as the foreground, then he will see a picture of facing profiles; but if he places the black area as the background and the white area as the foreground, he will see a picture of a vase.

That this single figure can signify in two ways suggests Locke was mistaken in believing a presented sense experience can add up to only one object, or unity. For here, a single datum presents two possible unities; and once this principle is grasped, it is possible to conceive of a datum that might yield three, four, five, or many more possible unities. It would appear, then, that the meaning of sense experiences can be grounded not in Lockean real objects, such as real apples and real drizzly rains, but in different intuitional configurations of the sensory field. Imagine, for example, the variety of configurations Picasso or Wallace Stevens could derive from Locke's simple apples and drizzly rains! Meaning can be taken as a contextual rather than an objective phenomenon.

I believe this is Shelley's way, although his Platonizing language, particularly in the *Defence*, often makes him appear to be a transcendentalist. He has to use such language because his cul-

ture has not evolved other terms that could conceptualize the force
and shape of his poetic intuitions. Unlike Picasso and Stevens,
he does not live in a culture that already has a sophisticated and
even weary awareness that human beings are forever creating their
own contexts. To him, this kind of experience is a revelation,
and he describes it in language that on the surface seems to be the
language of Platonic enthusiasm. But when such language is
analyzed, its description of form generally turns out to be psychological, not ontological. Here is an example from the *Defence*:

> A poem is the image of life expressed in its eternal truth.
> There is this difference between a story and a poem, that a
> story is a catalogue of detached facts, which have no other
> bond of connexion than time, place, circumstance, cause and
> effect; the other is the creation of actions according to the
> unchangeable forms of human nature, as existing in the mind
> of the creator, which is itself the image of all other minds.
> The one is partial, and applies only to a definite period of
> time, and a certain combination of events which can never
> again recur; the other is universal, and contains within itself
> the germ of a relation to whatever motives or actions have
> place in the possible varieties of human nature. Time, which
> destroys the beauty and the use of the story of particular
> facts, stript of the poetry which should invest them, aug-
> ments that of Poetry, and for ever develops new and
> wonderful applications of the eternal truth which it contains.
>
> (VII, 115)

Although it may look transcendental, this passage relies only upon
a distinction between serial and intuitional cognition. Serial experience delivers stories, catalogues of "detached facts, which have
no other bond of connexion than time, place, circumstance,
cause and effect." In other words, stories are organized by their
mode of mere step-by-step presentation, which is not a method
that creates meaning. But poems reveal "the unchangeable forms
of human nature" that can be extracted from stories, and which

give them a meaning that transcends their special facts. Such meanings go beyond particular circumstances not by being transcendental, but by providing an intuitional form that transforms our experiences. Just as we see a perceptual field that can be construed as an image of facing profiles or as a vase, so we consider a specific story that can be construed as a representative type of human experience—an "unchangeable form of human nature."

For Shelley, such representative types are experienced as images; and although his prose frequently makes these images sound like Platonic Forms, actually they function psychologically, as the form embodying his intuitions. Intuitive experience has to be radically compressive since it comes all at once; and therefore its formulation is apt to be by imagery, which is a medium that can express a large range of potential meaning through a single impression, or a brief flurry of impressions. So it is not surprising that in the *Defence* Shelley frequently employs the terms "image" and "picture," and also relies heavily upon imagery such as that of wind-lyres, veils, fading coals, and fountains to convey his intuitions about poetic experience. In the passage where he distinguishes between stories and poetry he says, "A poem is the *image* of life expressed in its eternal truth"; also, he remarks that "the mind of the creator . . . is itself the *image* of all other minds." A paragraph above this, he claims that the words of poets "unveil the permanent analogy of things by *images* which participate in the life of truth" (VII, 115; my emphasis). Furthermore, he makes a rather curious observation about Milton that makes sense only if an imagistic theory of poetic experience is assumed. He says that "Milton conceived the Paradise Lost as a whole before he executed it in portions" (VII, 136). In arguing that Milton originally created his epic "as a whole," Shelley cannot mean that the poet instantaneously composed the complete serial flow of words that constitute his poem; what he may mean is that Milton intuited *Paradise Lost* in some form that could be revealed as a unity. This form is the image—"the image of life expressed in its eternal truth"—the intuitive form that embodies a representative type of human experience.

But such images do not exist in the timeless safety of a transcendental heaven. To realize that Shelley's theory of imagery is not Platonic we need only to remind ourselves of the crucial significance assigned to the human cultural tradition in the *Defence*: it is man's civilization, rather than a transcendental realm, that hosts poetic images. Shelley was provoked into writing the *Defence* by Thomas Love Peacock's *The Four Ages of Poetry*, a hyperbolic exercise which denied Shelley's claim that culture is fundamentally a structure of poetic images, instead proposing that it is a march of scientific progress which illuminates real facts about the universe. For Peacock, poets in modern times have become peripheral figures because poetry is an endeavor that plays fast and loose with facts and thus is only credible in primitive ages. Contemporary poets necessarily are reduced to "the rant of unregulated passion, the whining of exaggerated feeling, and the cant of factitious sentiment"—drained of the solid fact which has been appropriated by science, their poetry becomes mere vacuous emotion.[6]

In reply, Shelley asserted that it is not Peacock's scientists and utilitarians who are the heroes of civilization, but the poets—and precisely because poets deal in imagination rather than unvarnished fact. Shelley does not place a high value on "objective" knowledge, with which he feels his culture already is overloaded: "We want the creative faculty to imagine that which we know; we want the generous impulse to act that which we imagine; we want the poetry of life: our calculations have outrun conception; we have eaten more than we can digest" (VII, 134). In other words, what we lack is intuitive knowledge—the understanding of what we know. This is what makes us human, what makes a society into a civilization. If Peacock can envision the scientists marching forward, irresistibly clearing out the underbrush,

Shelley can see no such inevitability in the poetry of civilization. At times (such as the fourth century in Athens) man can be supremely civilized; but at other times (such as, in Shelley's opinion, Restoration England) his humanity and civility atrophy.

What Shelley sees is not a triumphant march of poetry, but the constant effort of poets to humanize their societies. This effort must be unremitting, because no matter what success particular poets may enjoy, the images they create are entrusted to the cultural tradition; and instead of shining through with unsullied Platonic magnificence, these images very well may degenerate if the culture's mode of perception itself degenerates. When it is new, the language of poets "is vitally metaphorical; that is, it marks the before unapprehended relations of things and perpetuates their apprehension." But as time goes by, the novel formulations of poetry become familiar, and eventually are incorporated into our cultural habit patterns. Then such poetry becomes "signs for portions or classes of thoughts instead of pictures of integral thoughts" (VII, 111). For the reader, this poetry has become a cultural artifact so familiar that he no longer can intuit it as a living thing. The image that had been a vital "picture" has been thinned and abstracted until it has become a "sign," a shadow of its former self. Unless new poets come along to refresh the culture's perceptions and so renew its capacity for feeling experience, human life itself will become shadowy and stale.[7]

Just as a culture forever requires new poets to refresh its life, it also forever requires new readers. For although the poetry of past ages may appear to have degenerated from a living "picture" into a denatured "sign," it can be renewed by a novel reading. This is because poetry is not an "object" or "thing" that signifies one real meaning, but an experiential field that constantly lends itself to new constructions. The way to make dead poetry live is to lend one's own life to it. And so, "A great poem is a fountain for ever overflowing with the waters of wisdom and delight; and after one person and one age has exhausted all its divine effluence which their peculiar relations enable them to share, another and yet another succeeds, and new relations are ever developed, the source of an unforeseen and unconceived delight" (VII, 131).[8]

Thus, the famous Shelleyan "great poem which all poets, like the co-operating thoughts of one great mind, have built up since the beginning of the world" (VII, 124) is not a transcendental Form, but the continual transformation of our cultural past into the present, a process that must go on as long as we wish our culture to remain alive. In this sense, the whole of the human past is an immense perceptual field from which "pictures of integral thoughts" continually are emerging, only to attenuate and be reformed. The poet and the reader inherit the entire panorama of the past, but it will be useless to them unless they succeed in transforming its imagery into the forms revealed through their own living experience. In one sense, for Shelley, culture is massive and authoritative since he sees it as the main source of human experience; but in another sense, it is perilously frail and in need of nourishment—for it lives or dies continuously, in the transforming sensibilities of living persons. The Shelleyan images exist not in heaven but in evolving human consciousness.[9]

As an example of this Shelleyan cultural process, consider "Ozymandias" (1817), a poem in which the speaker brings the human past alive within his present reflections:[10]

> I met a traveller from an antique land
> Who said: Two vast and trunkless legs of stone
> Stand in the desert . . . Near them, on the sand,
> Half sunk, a shattered visage lies, whose frown,
> And wrinkled lip, and sneer of cold command,
> Tell that its sculptor well those passions read
> Which yet survive, stamped on these lifeless things,
> The hand that mocked them, and the heart that fed:
> And on the pedestal these words appear:
> "My name is Ozymandias, king of kings:
> Look on my works, ye Mighty, and despair!"

> Nothing beside remains. Round the decay
> Of that colossal wreck, boundless and bare
> The lone and level sands stretch far away.[11]

Here "The hand that mocked them, and the heart that fed" do
not, I think, belong to the same person. The heart is that of the
tyrant Ozymandias; but the hand is the sculptor's—a hand which
has transformed that terrible heart's passions into a grim "visage."
By so doing, the artist has "mocked" the king, for instead of
producing a self-congratulatory political monument to feed Ozymandias' passions, in this terrible face he has created an image of
the tyrant's debased heart—an image which is at once a true
portrait of Ozymandias and also the very representative type of
tyranny. But presumably Ozymandias was too vain to perceive
the artistic context from which this uncomplimentary vision of
himself emerges; so that in the king's own time this statue was
allowed to stand, seemingly a testimony to regal power, but to
the perceptive viewer, actually a condemnation of tyranny.

Ages later when Shelley's traveller sees the statue, it has
crumbled away, and Ozymandias' graven words, "My name is
Ozymandias, king of kings:/ Look on my works, ye Mighty, and
despair!" have assumed a new meaning, because they are now
perceived through the unforgiving, monument-destroying context of time. Ironically, instead of asserting temporal power,
Ozymandias' own statement now denies the very possibility of it.
The tyrant's city, which must have surrounded his statue, has
disappeared completely, replaced by the "boundless and bare"
sands; and his effigy lies dismembered, a scattering of "trunkless
legs" and "shattered visage." But the scowling face lying half-
buried in the sand still speaks of the corruption of tyranny as
clearly as the day it was sculpted. Although the words and works
of Ozymandias are ruined by age, the truth perceived by the
unknown artist is carried intact through time, by the power of his
imagery.

All these insights emerge from the framing context of a story, for the sonnet's speaker himself has not seen Ozymandias' ancient city; he has heard about it from "a traveller from an antique land." The poem's contexts are like a set of nesting Chinese boxes: a vision has been transmitted by the sculptor who made the image, to the traveller who saw it, to the speaker who hears about it, to the reader of the poem, who overheard the speaker's lyrical meditation. But this line of communication, person to person and age to age, can remain unbroken only if all the individuals involved in it have the power of insight. Although the image of Ozymandias drawn by the sonnet suggests that artistic power is greater, and more enduring, than the power of any tyrant, this claim can be supported only so long as people exist who have the perceptiveness to see its truth. Thus, Shelley's assertion of man's freedom in "Ozymandias" is distinctly not transcendental: freedom is a capacity of soul that must live or die in the sensibilities of every generation. Although the right to freedom has been nobly asserted in the past by the sculptor, by the traveller who passes, and by the composer of the sonnet, the real experience of freedom now rests upon every reader of "Ozymandias": do we have the perceptiveness to bring alive the "picture" embedded in this poem, or will it be a sterile "sign" for us? If it is, we will be precisely as dead to the vision of freedom as was Ozymandias himself.

But if the reader can see the sonnet as a vital "picture," he will have the privilege of construing an image of much greater scope and richness than the one available to the original artist. As Shelley said in the *Defence*, "Time, which destroys the beauty and the use of the story of particular facts   augments that of Poetry, and for ever develops new and wonderful applications of the eternal truth which it contains." In "Ozymandias," time has enhanced the sculptor's portrait by adding the barren sands, the shattered trunk and legs of the statue, and the ironic conversion of Ozymandias' words as details that confirm and enrich the artist's original image. Next, the traveller's appreciative perception of these elements has been intensified and focused by the poetic speaker's language. In fact, the perceptive reader is privileged to witness three works of art, the last two dependent upon the prior ones and in turn progressively expanding their scope: at the center of Shelley's full vision is the sculptor's image of Ozymandias, but around it is the halo of the traveller's story, with its description of the fragmented statue and surrounding sands; and enclosing all this is the speaker's poetic transformation of these forms into the discipline of the sonnet. In "Ozymandias" the past becomes a perceptual field that continually enlarges with the passage of time, creating possibilities for the continual artistic transformation of the image focused at its center.

But no matter how many contextual frames or halos a poetic vision may receive, no matter how many transformations it may undergo, for Shelley the situation portrayed in "Ozymandias" always will hold true: at the center of everything will be an image, the visible symbol of an intuitional integration of experience. As artists continue to reexperience this image, it will continue to transform—to be renewed and enriched. This seems to me the theme that unites Shelley's major poetry, and the readings in this volume work toward demonstration of that view.

I have chosen *The Transforming Image* as my title because I want to emphasize that Shelley's imagery is transformational, not transcendental. I call this image "transforming," rather than "transformed," to stress that Shelleyan transformation is an open-ended process, an act that must be continuous in order to perpetuate its own existence.[12] The Shelleyan world necessarily is a world of constant movement; the penalty implied in cessation of movement is death, the reduction of the living poetic "picture" into an attenuated "sign." In the next chapter I turn to *Alastor*, the seminal poem in which Shelley implies this need for incessant transformation by telling the story of a Poet whose imagery fails to transform. The Poet's static response to his dream image becomes a self-destructive fixation that literally causes his death.

NOTES

1. W. T. Jones, *A History of Western Philosophy* (New York, 1952), p. 730.

2. David Hume, *A Treatise of Human Nature* (1739), Book I, part IV, section vi, "Of personal identity."

3. William Godwin, *An Enquiry Concerning Political Justice* (1793); William Drummond, *Academical Questions* (1805). For an account of Godwin's and Drummond's influence on Shelley, see C. E. Pulos, *The Deep Truth: A Study of Shelley's Skepticism* (Lincoln, Nebr., 1954, 1962).

4. *The Complete Works of Percy Bysshe Shelley*, ed. Roger Ingpen and Walter E. Peck, Julian edition, 10 vols. (London and New York, 1926–30). Unless otherwise stated, all references to Shelley's prose—except for his letters and the prefaces to his poems—are based on this edition and will be noted by volume and page number in the text.

5. Edgar Rubin, *Synsoplevede Figurer: Studier i psykologisk Analyse* (Copenhagen, 1915).

6. *Shelley's Critical Prose*, ed. Bruce R. McElderry, Jr. (Lincoln, Nebr., 1967), p. 170.

7. John W. Wright rather nicely terms this phenomenon "semantic entropy." See *Shelley's Myth of Metaphor* (Athens, Ga., 1970), p. 29 ff.

8. Considering this aspect of the *Defence*, it is not surprising that it can be easily adapted to a structuralist reading. See Robert Scholes, "Romantic and Structuralist Theories of Poetic Language," *Structuralism in Literature: An Introduction* (New Haven and London, 1974), pp. 170–80.

9. Hans-Georg Gadamer's analysis of culture as a dialogue between past and present that results in a "fusion of horizons" shows interesting resemblances to Shelley's vision of culture in "Ozymandias." See *Truth and Method* (New York, 1975).

10. "The Greek author Diodorus Siculus lived in the Nile Valley from 60 to 57 B.C. and was one of the first people to write about the huge seated figures of Amenophis III on the floodplain at Thebes. The Greeks named these spectacular statues the Colossi of Memnon, after a Homeric hero. Ramesses II's nearby temple, the Ramesseum, became known as the Memnonium. Diodorus admired the Ramesseum and its courts with its statues of the king. He found an inscription on one of the figures, which he quoted, attributing the temple correctly to Ozymandias, the Greek equivalent of User-ma'et-Re, the actual name of Ramesses II: 'My name is is Ozymandias, king of kings; if any would know how great I am and

where I lie, let him surpass me in any of my works.'" Brian M. Fagan, *The Rape of the Nile: Tomb Robbers, Tourists, and Archaeologists in Egypt* (New York, 1975), p. 23.

11. *Complete Poetical Works of Percy Bysshe Shelley*, ed. Thomas Hutchinson (New York, 1951). Unless otherwise stated, all references to Shelley's poetry and to prefaces to poems are based on this edition.

12. Interestingly, Jerome J. McGann uses Platonic terminology in his reading of Shelley, but comes to the very unPlatonic conclusion that, in effect, Shelley avoids encountering the Absolute, preferring forever to remain in a world of transforming appearances. I concur with this conclusion, but in this volume I will try to show that a nonPlatonic vocabulary describes the transformational properties of Shelleyan poetry more adequately than does McGann's. See Jerome J. McGann, "Shelley's Veils: A Thousand Images of Loveliness," in *Romantic and Victorian: Studies in Memory of William H. Marshall*, ed. W. Paul Elledge and Richard L. Hoffman (Rutherford, N.J., 1971), pp. 198–217. From pps. 214 and 217: "No one image of Life or a condition of Life—no one group of images—can be allowed a definitiveness. The Epipsyche, and the One, require a universe of imaginative fragments in an eternity of time to exhibit their full loveliness. . . . Language is a veiled vision, and the poet's veil of imagery must be destroyed if the power of vision is to be sustained, if fresh creations are to be brought forth and new figured curtains to be woven. . . . because the deep truth is imageless, the imagination rises to upbuild itself into ever new forms, and only by describing this endlessly generative process does it approximate the ideal source of all generation and power. Thus, the imagination is both a veiling and an unveiling power."

CHAPTER TWO

The Struggle to Transform Experience:
Alastor and "Hymn to Intellectual Beauty"

Alastor is Shelley's first effective treatment of the most frequently recurring theme in his poetry—the theme of the promising young wanderer, the inspired solitary who is forever on the move, searching the world for the person or experience that could fulfill the needs of his idealism. As Shelley remarks in *On Life*, which probably was written before or about the time of *Alastor*, ". . . man is a being of high aspirations, 'looking both before and after,' whose 'thoughts wander through eternity,' disclaiming alliance with transience and decay; incapable of imagining to himself annihilation; existing but in the future and the past; being, not what he is, but what he has been and shall be. Whatever may be his true and final destination, there is a spirit within him at enmity with nothingness and dissolution" (VI, 194). Man essentially is an idealist, and idealists are seekers, wanderers, pilgrims who hope someday to find something in the world worthy of their own high imaginings. Thus, the *Alastor* Poet: we learn that

"When early youth had passed, he left/ His cold fireside and
alienated home/ To seek strange truths in undiscovered lands"
(75–77). Why his home was alienated is never explained; presumably, that is simply the nature of homes, a conclusion that
Shelley must have found easy to draw from his personal experience. As soon as a youth is old enough, he must leave home to
wander, to move forever in search of an undefined something that
is his heart's desire and his real home. As the poem's epigraph
from St. Augustine says, *Nondum amabam, et amare amabam,
quaerebam quid amarem, amans amare* (Not yet did I love, yet I loved
to love; I sought something to love, being in love with love).[1]

In his Preface to *Alastor* Shelley claims that as long as the
wandering Poet contemplates "The magnificence and beauty of
the external world" his mind retains the scope for continual
expansion: "the frame of his conceptions" is modified in "a variety not to be exhausted. So long as it is possible for his desires to
point toward objects thus infinite and unmeasured, he is joyous,
and tranquil, and self-possessed." His trouble begins when in a
dream "He images to himself the Being whom he loves." Unfortunately for the Poet, precisely because this image is measured
by himself, it cannot be "infinite and unmeasured." As the poem
tells us, his dream lady sings with a voice "like the voice of his
own soul/ Heard in the calm of thought; its music . . . held/ His
inmost sense. . . . Thoughts the most dear to him, and poesy,/
Herself a poet" (153–61). His dream, then, is a primitive unconscious transformation: he has created an image that is himself but
not himself—the best of himself, transformed into the form of
woman. His "infinite and unmeasured" desires are contracted to
one center; as the Preface says, "The intellectual faculties, the
imagination, the functions of sense have their respective requisitions. . . . The Poet is represented as uniting these requisitions,
and attaching them to a single image."

But unlike the sculptor's portrait in "Ozymandias," this cen-
tered image does not continue to transform through time. Perhaps

if this had happened, the Poet's desire for the "infinite and unmeasured" might have been satisfied by "a variety not to be
exhausted." Instead, the Poet mistakes the image for reality, and
"reared his shuddering limbs and quelled/ His gasping breath, and
spread his arms to meet/ Her panting bosom" (182–84). Quite
literally he plunges into the center of the image, in an attempt at a
totally abandoned erotic union.[2] But the result is not the kind of
orgasmic fusion praised in the *Defence*, where the poet "participates in the eternal, the infinite, and the one; as far as relates to his
conceptions, time and place and number are not" (VII, 112).
Instead, the lady's "dissolving arms" also dissolve the Poet's mind;
"Now blackness veiled his dizzy eyes, . . . sleep . . . Rolled back
its impulse on his vacant brain" (187–91). The moment of fusion
has been so intense that it overstrains the Poet's faculties, and he
blacks out.

Ironically, this unrestrained attempt to embrace the image now
leads to an abolition of the Poet's very powers of imagery. When
he wakes, he finds that for him nature has become a perceptual
field that no longer yields significant configurations. "Whither
have fled/ The hues of heaven . . . The mystery and the majesty of
Earth,/ The joy, the exultation? His wan eyes/ Gaze on the scene
as vacantly/ As ocean's moon looks on the moon in heaven" (196–
202). The capacity for imagery depends upon the mind's ability
to structure fields, but this Poet's eyes and mind have become like
a reflection of the moon in the ocean—they only can replicate,
not formulate, things. In fact, we could say that the Poet himself
now is a kind of image, instead of a maker of images. Like
Lockean man, he is a mirror that accurately reflects the flow of his
phenomenal experience but has no power to construe it. Before
his vision the Poet wandered eagerly, in pursuit of the "variety"
of meanings "not to be exhausted" in nature. Afterward his
wanderings are an attempt not at discovery, but at escape from a
fallen state in which his life and world fail to show meaning.
Instead of an idealistic quest, the Poet's wandering becomes a

feverish restlessness, an attempt to escape his empty and self-tormenting self.

And of course, the only complete escape is death. The Poet's idealistic vision, with its termination in his lady's "dissolving arms," at last leads literally to his dissolution. But before he dies, he pauses to contemplate his reflection in a still pool of water:

> His eyes beheld
> Their own wan light through the reflected lines
> Of his thin hair, distinct in the dark depth
> Of that still fountain; as the human heart,
> Gazing in dreams over the gloomy grave,
> Sees its own treacherous likeness there.
>
> (469–74)

If his image of the lady was an unconscious idealistic transformation, this mirror image of himself is its ironic counterpart: a self-conscious degenerative recognition—the moment when he realizes that his feverish despair has ruined his body, and he accepts his impending death. The poem suggests that the human potential for transformation is polar: either it can create ideals or it can lead to destruction. As Shelley says of another poetical wanderer in "The Sunset," written the year after *Alastor*, "There late was One within whose subtle being/ . . . Genius and death contended."

It is because intense visions can bring death that Shelley shows himself so afraid of them in *Alastor*. He attempts to distance the Poet's dangerous experience by recounting it through the eyes of a narrator, a poetic soul who once sought the kind of intensity embraced by the Poet, but who has learned to moderate his desires before they destroyed him. This narrator advocates a passive Wordsworthian receptivity to the influences of Mother Nature: "serenely now/ And moveless . . . I wait thy breath, Great Parent" (41–45).[3] Her creatures become his "kindred" and "belovèd brethren" (15–18), and he exists within a benevolent familial relationship. But the Poet's attempt at erotic consummation raises questions about the narrator's identification of himself as Nature's "child": does he join the natural family out of love, or because he is afraid of fully adult experience and hopes to be protected from it by the mother?

His relationship to the Poet raises a similar question. Although he suggests that *Alastor* is a sort of cautionary tale, an illustration of how poets can go wrong, clearly he admires the Poet who is the center of his story. In fact, if Nature is the narrator's mother, the Poet can be seen as his spiritual father—the totally committed genius he wishes, but fears, to be. The narrator is not really a poet precisely because he is a man of caution, dedicated primarily to his own preservation and only secondarily to his visions. But despite all his care, in the end the narrator does not succeed in protecting himself. After his admired Poet has died, he sees the corpse as "An image, silent, cold and motionless,/ As . . . voiceless earth and vacant air" (661–62) and cries in despair, "It is a woe too 'deep for tears,' when all/ Is reft at once . . . Nature's vast frame, the web of human things,/ Birth and the grave, . . . are not as they were" (713–20). For this narrator, nature suddenly is emptied of its significance by the Poet's death exactly as, for the Poet, it was suddenly emptied of significance by the disappearance of his visionary lady. If the lady has been the Poet's idealized self-image, in turn, the Poet has been the narrator's idealized self-image. In the end, the brotherhood of nature turns out to be inadequate because the fundamental human need is relationship with another human being.

But a loving relationship with other human beings is precisely what *Alastor* portrays as impossible. The Poet ignores the Arab maid who loves him, because he can be interested only in an idealized transformation of himself; and the narrator unsuccessfully tries to hold back from identification with the Poet because he loves his own life better than the poetic ideal. For all their differences, the motivations of the Poet and the narrator betray a similar taint of selfishness—what the Preface terms "self-centered seclusion." This is why Peacock's title is apt, even though it was suggested after Shelley's poem was finished: "At this time, Shelley wrote his *Alastor*. He was at a loss for a title, and I proposed that which he adopted: *Alastor, or the Spirit of Solitude*. The Greek word is an evil genius. . . . The poem treated the spirit of solitude as a spirit of evil. I mention the true meaning of the word because many have supposed Alastor to be the name of the hero of the poem."[4] In the end, *Alastor* is a poem of solitude, its images a claustrophobic hall of mirrors that eternally reflect the self—the loved and hated self, the self we transform into our ideal and the self we seek death in order to escape.[5]

At this point I will go beyond an analysis of *Alastor* to indulge in some speculations on the dilemma of "self-centering" that it poses. As far as I can see, *Alastor* confines itself to a strong presentation of the problem; it offers no solutions. But I can imagine a Shelleyan way out of this impasse, a way that is consistent with the later poetry discussed in this volume.

It is not necessarily the visions of the Poet and the narrator that cause their troubles; it is how they construe them. Both characters are naive realists who expect their visions to be revelations of things that enjoy an existence independent of their own perceptions. Thus, the Poet reaches out toward the image he has created, in a literal attempt to embrace it; and in his salad days the narrator "made . . . magic" and acted "Like an inspired and desperate alchymist" (36–37, 31) in an attempt to possess nature's secrets by force. Interestingly, what he wants to conjure up is "the tale/ Of what we are" (28–29), as though our identity were an objective "something" separate from our consciousness of it. In this sense the Poet's effort to grasp his visionary lady and the narrator's magical quest to grasp what he really is exemplify the same impulse: both characters attempt to embrace transformed versions of themselves.

It is important here to stress the "transformed"; for clearly, neither the Poet nor the narrator feels sufficient unto himself. The one begins a life of wandering and the other begins a life of writing precisely because something more than the self is felt to be necessary; and their movement is a movement toward what might satisfy desire. What they require is not themselves merely, but selves that at the same time are different from and yet the same as themselves. In his Preface to *Alastor* Shelley remarked that the poem "may be considered as allegorical of one of the most interesting situations of the human mind," and surely he is right—at any rate, *Alastor* portrays one of the situations most interesting to the Romantic mind. Many of the great Romantic careers focus here: think of Chateaubriand's *René*, Byron's *Manfred*, Keats's *Endymion*, Rousseau's *Julie*, and the most famous of them all, Goethe's *The Sorrows of Young Werther*. Like *Alastor*, all these works portray a young idealist who fails to find scope in life for exerting his unusual powers of love. Thwarted in his desire, the protagonist either dies or commits suicide, or somehow is rescued. In all of these cases the young man loves or wishes for a woman who answers to the *Alastor* archetype: someone not himself, but like himself—himself transformed into the form of woman. The notorious Romantic interest in incest is a special version of this.

One Romantic strategy for dealing with the situation is to write about it: the act of writing becomes a substitute for the act of loving.[6] Although the following remarks from Goethe's autobiography are not specifically about the torments of Romantic ideal love, they do suggest how writing could function to relieve its stresses: "And so, there began that tendency, which I could never deviate from all my life, to turn what delighted or tortured or otherwise occupied me into an image or a poem and be done with it, both in order to correct my notions of outer things, and to compose myself inwardly. No one needed this gift more than I, because my nature flung me continually from one extreme to the

other. Thus, all my works are fragments of a great confession. . . ."[7] The Romantic confession, then, is a transformation: the tormented or ecstatic self transformed into forms of self-
revelation—a transformation that allays desire.

But this general solution is not adequate for the Poet of *Alastor*, its narrator, or for Shelley himself. In writing *Alastor* Shelley
has adopted the strategy of his narrator, which is writing about his
torment in order to distance it—a solution not unlike the one
described above by Goethe. This, at least, offers some possibilities
for control not explored by the archetypal Poet, who as far as the
poem tells us, never has written a line! But Alastor demonstrates
that, at best, its narrator's stance only holds the problem temporarily at bay. The visions of *Alastor* suggest that the wished-for
Shelleyan solution involves release rather than substitution—ecstatic union with one's own imagery.

But this is impossible as long as Shelley maintains his own
Poet's attitude toward visionary experience—that is, as long as he
construes it as transcendental. If the beloved actually exists, then
clearly she exists in a world entirely separate from his own, where
she never can be touched by him. If Shelley is to possess his
visions in the uncompromising way he desires, he must cease to
regard them as real objects existing outside his poetry; and conversely, cease to regard poetry as a substitute for whatever it is
that he really desires. His poetry must become all in all for him:
the dualistic world inevitably posited by transcendentalist philoso-
phies, a world constituted of Appearance and Reality, must
become a single world. For him, poetic appearance must be
everything. In such a world, the pursuit of one's visionary beloved may end in an orgasmic embrace, if appearances can be
transformed into the kind of world that can host one's visions.
The beloved can become one's own only when the world itself
becomes one's own. At bottom, then, the *Alastor* Poet's quest is
for himself: he seeks his own self, but transformed into a world.

This is another way of saying that, if he only had realized it, he really was in pursuit of a poem.

If the dilemmas of *Alastor* suggest the transformational kind of poem that Shelley needed to write, the "Hymn to Intellectual Beauty," written the following year, is the first effective example of that kind of poem. Here we are privileged to witness the transforming image not as a seemingly real object hopelessly sought for, but as a poetic element that exists strictly within the world of the poem.

However, it is true that like the Poet of *Alastor*, the speaker of the "Hymn to Intellectual Beauty" begins his poem enmeshed in seemingly transcendental urgencies. Just as the Poet has envisioned a lover not to be discovered in the world, so this speaker describes an elusive feminine Spirit of Beauty that beckons from the unknown. In *Alastor* this kind of transcendental interest led both to the Poet's rejection of the world and to the unresolved, unreleased quality of the poem itself. The advance beyond these attitudes created in the "Hymn" turns upon the poet's new ability to see his poem as an imaginary equivalent of the world—as a poetic world that might be transformed by his poetic powers. Now, instead of focusing his attention toward something "real" beyond the poem, the speaker can employ his energies in transforming the world of the poem until it approaches the form of his desires. In the "Hymn to Intellectual Beauty" the naive transcendentalism that permeates *Alastor* is converted into a kind of potentially sophisticated poetic transformation. Shelley's literal urges have been transformed into poetic ones. Consequently, the technical form of his poems begins to be of great interest, and it is to these features of the "Hymn" that I now turn.

The poem begins with the astonishing Shelleyan abundance of imagery that also initiates such poems as "To a Skylark" and *Epipsychidion*: in the first four stanzas there is a flood of metaphor,

necessitated by the fact that Beauty, the subject of the poem, is
an "unseen Power" (1) that can be described only by comparing it
with what can be seen or otherwise sensed.[8] Clearcut metaphorical phrases are signaled by the words "as" (3–4), "like" (5, 8, 9,
10, 11, 32, 37, 45, 47), "or," which extends the force of "like" in
line 32 to 33 and then to 35, and "why" (18, 20, 21, 23). Thus,
there are sixteen overt metaphors in the poem's first forty-eight
lines; but beyond that, the entire language of this passage is
metaphorically based. In effect, the poet can find no way to
discuss his subject other than by indirection. We may be tempted
to say that it all is too much, that such a superabundance of
random comparisons can lead only to confusion. And so it does—
at first. However, what this fecundity produces is a large poetic
field containing many small images but no overall picture. What
the copious fragmentary imagery allows for is the possibility of a
large coalescence.

Indeed, we can see that at least to some extent the comparisons
do have an underlying theme: ten of the sixteen involve light
and darkness. Beauty, which in an additional covert metaphor,
"shine(s) upon" us and has "hues" (14), is also "Like moonbeams
that behind some piny mountain shower" (5), or "Like hues and
harmonies of evening," or "Like clouds in starlight widely
spread" (8–9). Its departure is like the vanishing of "rainbows o'er
yon mountain river" (19); like light, it can "fail and fade" (20),
and it resembles "moonlight on a midnight stream" (35). The
cumulative implication is that Beauty can be identified with light,
and its absence can be associated with darkness; for when Beauty
departs, this world becomes a "dim vast vale of tears, vacant and
desolate" (17), and then we see "Cast on the daylight of this earth/
Such gloom" (22–23).

Apparently, light and darkness function as metaphors for ex-
hilaration and depression. These polar states seem to be inherent
in the human condition: one is either approaching one's dream or

bereft of it, as in *Alastor*; man has an immense "scope/ For love and hate, despondency and hope" (23–24). The imagery which expresses this oscillation emphasizes its quicksilver unpredictability. Comparisons of Beauty's visitations to such things as "moonbeams that behind some piny mountain shower" (5) or "moonlight on a midnight stream" (35) involve evanescent aspects of moonlight—moonbeams coming from behind a mountain, so as to silhouette it, light reflected in a stream—which have, in the moon itself, a solid cause. This imagery suggests that the speaker has access to the flickering appearances of nature but not to the steady hidden forces which create them. No wonder he longs for "Self-esteem" as well as "Love" and "Hope" (37): like the *Alastor* Poet he feels powerless, the victim of life's mutability. He is at once the source of his own hope and despair, forever reeling between visions of Beauty and vacancies of depression.

In stanza V he describes one of these intuitions of Beauty experienced in his childhood, which had such force that it resembled a religious conversion. Like the *Alastor* Poet's dream vision, this experience has changed his life; and like that dream, it possessed him unawares: "Sudden, thy shadow fell on me;/ I shrieked, and clasped my hands in extacy!" But it is Beauty's "shadow," not its illumination, that falls upon the child, and this is odd in a poem that hitherto has equated Beauty with light. This puzzle is clarified by an image in stanza IV. There the speaker says Beauty is "to human thought . . . nourishment,/ Like darkness to a dying flame!" (44–45). At first this curious image does not stand out; but when one stops to think about it, the only way darkness can "nourish" a flame is by suddenly descending around it so that the flame appears to flare into brightness through dramatic contrast with the black background.

Clearly, something rather like this has happened during the child's vision. He has experienced Beauty not as an external force,

but as a sudden interior illumination. Indeed, his intuitional experience has been strong enough to suddenly transpose the entire
context of his world vision. At the foreground of his experience
has been the assumption that Beauty is a hidden entity transcend-
ing "This various world" (3)—something that hides behind
appearances and is their cause; something, therefore, that must be
pursued with the utmost heroism of the human will. But in his
moment of great intuition, Beauty is experienced as a background
condition that suddenly emerges into the foreground through
himself, the descent of an unwilled and unwillable state of mind in
which he has visionary power.

As the speaker's vision was once transformed in his childhood,
so the poem's imagery also has undergone a transformation that
allows the reminiscing adult to reformulate his experience, both
past and present. The first four stanzas of the "Hymn" have
suggested that Beauty is like light and depression is like darkness;
but this assumption is transformed by the image of Beauty as a
darkness descending upon the dying flame of the human mind.
Vacancy, depression, the dark drifting states in which self-control
is surrendered, can be valuable after all. They may be the enabling condition for intuitive visions. Beauty is light, then, insofar
as it is an illumination, but darkness, insofar as it is a mysterious
and uncompellable enabling condition. In grasping what the *Defence* would call this previously "unapprehended combination of
thought," the speaker has transformed the poem's entire perceptual field. The random metaphors of the poem's first four stanzas
suddenly have been changed by their placement within a definitive
context of imagery. The poem remains metaphorical but is no
longer a congeries of small comparisons: now it presents one
clear, consistent picture.

In *Alastor* the transforming image was the Poet's dream lover,
the nebulous transcendental presence he never could embrace; in
the "Hymn" the transforming image has become a poetic ele-

ment, the expressive mirror that allows the poet to examine himself, to formulate his own feeling.

This device is wonderfully appropriate for Shelley's purpose because it operates within the structure of the poem very much as our moments of inspiration operate in life. The speaker is dealing with a childhood experience in which he suddenly felt changed; the poem that the adult writes enacts this change artistically by building up a trend of imagery, which at the climactic point suddenly is transformed. This procedure is typical of the world view Stephen C. Pepper calls organicism, which involves these categories: "(1) fragments of experience which appear with (2) *nexuses* or connections or implications, which spontaneously lead as a result of the aggravation of (3) *contradictions*, gaps, oppositions, or counteractions to resolution in (4) an *organic whole*, which is found to have been (5) *implicit* in the fragments, and to (6) *transcend* the previous contradictions by means of a coherent totality, which (7) *economizes*, saves, preserves all the original fragments of experience without any loss."[9] As a poetic structure, the "Hymn" shows the progress expressed in Pepper's categories. Copious metaphors which (1) appear as fragmentary attempts to codify experience develop (2) nexuses or implications that Beauty is like light and darkness is like depression, but encounter (3) the contradiction that Beauty is also like "darkness to a dying flame," which leads to the resolution that (4 and 6) the organic whole which successfully incorporates both light and darkness transcends the previous metaphorical fragments by transforming them; but (5 and 7) this new formulation always has been an implicit possibility of the fragmentary metaphors and its actualization preserves all the material of the poem without any loss.

In particular, stanzas VI and VII show that there has been no loss in the metaphorical material of the poem, for images which earlier had expressed the speaker's lack of comprehension and control now are transformed to express his adequate grasp of things. As a child he futilely pursued ghosts, but now with satisfaction he can invoke the "phantoms of a thousand hours" spent not in hopeless quests but in "studious zeal or love's delight" (64, 66). What had been the unpredictable light of Beauty now is changed into a steadier illumination—the "solemn and serene" light of afternoon or the "harmony" and "lustre" of autumn's sky (73–75). The entire poem is transformed into a hymn that reveres not an external power but the mysteries within the speaker's own self. Taken properly, Beauty's spells bind him "To fear himself, and love all human kind" (84).

In fact, from this final vantage point we can see that in addressing his language of worship and love to Beauty, the speaker of the "Hymn" actually has been talking to himself. Like the *Alastor* Poet, who involuntarily creates a dream image that is an idealized transformation of himself, this speaker has imagined a beloved deity who is an idealized projection of his own divine powers. But to speak directly to oneself as a lover and a god would be a blasphemy far beyond the self-centeredness of the *Alastor* Poet. The speaker is able to retain his intimations of divinity and also a saving reverence and humility because his poetic speech creates a context in which his own powers become aspects of his imagined world—aspects which he sums up in the term "Beauty." The poem is a success because this speaker has been able to use his transformed self-image to express feelings that would have been both insufferably arrogant and fundamentally distorted if expressed in any other way. Where the *Alastor* Poet remained imprisoned within himself, this speaker's poetic expression has allowed for the release of a genuinely idealistic vision. The self-image that remained untransformed in *Alastor* is here transformed; and we see that this implies the entry into the world by the poet, his creation of a poetic universe that everywhere embodies his self.

Thus, the frustrated transcendentalism of *Alastor* is converted by the speaker of the "Hymn to Intellectual Beauty" into a species of poetic transformation. Although the "Hymn" is concerned with elusive powers, intimations of divinity, influences that can be felt but not quite expressed, the poem ultimately does not treat these forces as objective "things" that transcend its poetic scope in the way that the *Alastor* Poet treated his visionary lover as a real person who transcended the world. The speaker of the "Hymn" transforms his perceptual context, sees and speaks in a way that will allow his intuitions to come forth into his poem. This means, of course, that the poem itself must be a kind of fiction. But the fictional is not necessarily the false—and indeed, the very strength of the "Hymn" is a function of its obviously fictional character. For to interpret the poem literally, as the record of a relationship between a goddess named Beauty and a person named Percy Bysshe Shelley, is to trivialize it to the point of worthlessness.

I make this *reductio ad absurdum* case to throw into relief Shelley's notion of the relationship between life and art. For the later Shelley, art becomes a fiction that can tell truths sayable in no other way, and therefore it can extend our experience beyond the limits of our actual lives. It does so not by making real things and experiences available to us, as the *Alastor* Poet hoped to see his vision made flesh, but by expanding our fundamental capacity for experience, our human scope. Art delivers not objective truth but human enrichment; it succeeds not by grasping some external reality but by transforming its beholders. As Shelley says in the Preface to *Prometheus Unbound*: "My purpose has . . . been . . . to familiarize the highly refined imagination of the more select classes of poetical readers with beautiful idealisms of moral excellence; aware that until the mind can love, and admire, and trust, and hope, and endure, reasoned principles of moral conduct are seeds cast upon the highway of life which the unconscious passenger tramples into dust. . . ." Life and art are closely related for

Shelley, but emphatically, they are not an identity. Shelleyan art
is an inspired fiction that can deliver truths different than life's;
and so, to make the same truth claims for art and life could
amount to a kind of poetic tyranny—to the assertion that *what I
imagine must be the Truth*. A notable feature of Shelley's later poems
considered in this book is their incorporation of a kind of poetic
disclaimer, a questioning or a deliberate breaking of the context at
the end of each poem, which leads the reader to realize that he
has seen one poet's vision of the truth, not Truth itself. Within its
own context the Shelleyan poem creates enthusiastic belief in a
world of ideal possibility, and then by deliberately stepping outside this context the poet implicitly admits the possibility of other
visions, other experiences of the world, other ways of enlarging
the human scope.[10] The Shelleyan poem becomes valuable not
because of the particular imaginative experience it creates, but
more generally because it gives its readers the very experience of
imagination itself. So Shelley's later poetry becomes determinedly
anti-transcendental: it deals in experience, not objective truth.
"Mont Blanc" is the first of Shelley's poems to fully exhibit these
features, and the next poem to which I will turn.

NOTES

    1. Quoted and translated in Earl R. Wasserman, *Shelley: A Critical
Reading* (Baltimore, 1971), p. 17.
    2. The Platonist interpretation of Shelley has tended to idealize the
erotic passages in *Alastor* and *Epipsychidion*. For a rebuttal, see "Shelley's
'Alastor' and 'Epipsychidion'" in Gerald Enscoe, *Eros and the Romantics:
Sexual Love as a Theme in Coleridge, Shelley and Keats* (The Hague, 1967),
pp. 61–98.
    3. For discussions of Wordsworth's influence on *Alastor*, see Harold
Bloom, *The Visionary Company: A Reading of English Romantic Poetry*,
revised and enlarged edition (Ithaca, N.Y., 1971), pp. 285–90; and
Wasserman, *Shelley*, pp. 15–21.
    4. Thomas Love Peacock, *Memoirs of Shelley and Other Essays and
Reviews*, ed. Howard Mills (New York, 1970), p. 60.
    5. For an excellent discussion of the problem of "self-centering" in
Shelley, see Milton Wilson, "The Sphere of our Sorrow," in *Shelley's*

Later Poetry: A Study of His Prophetic Imagination (New York, 1959), pp. 148–70.

6. Jacques Derrida suggests that writing is an analogue of sexuality, and more specifically, that it is a transformation of what his translator terms "auto-affection." See *Of Grammatology*, trans. Gayatri Chakravorty Spivak (Baltimore and London, 1976), and especially part II, "Nature, Culture, Writing."

7. *The Autobiography of Johann Wolfgang von Goethe (Dichtung und Wahrheit)*, trans. John Oxenford, intro. Gregor Sebba (New York, 1969), p. 305 (Volume I, part Two, Book VII).

8. The text of the "Hymn" referred to in this chapter is from Judith Chernaik, *The Lyrics of Shelley* (Cleveland and London, 1972). For an account of the transcription of "Hymn to Intellectual Beauty" in Mary Shelley's hand discovered in the Scrope Davies find, see Judith Chernaik and Timothy Burnett, "The Byron and Shelley Notebooks in the Scrope Davies Find," *RES* new series, vol. xxxix, no. 113 (Feb. 1978), pp. 36–49.

9. Stephen C. Pepper, *World Hypotheses: A Study in Evidence* (Berkeley, Calif., 1942), p. 283.

10. Wasserman is well aware of the skeptical strain in Shelley's poetry, and even titles Part I of his *Shelley* "Skepticism." However, where I see Shelley's skepticism as involving the relationship of virtual experience as enacted in poetry to actual experience as enacted in life, Wasserman understands Shelley's poetry to be concerned with the investigation of ontological truth, and his skepticism to be involved with his awareness that poetry cannot definitively discover the nature of reality. From *Shelley*, p. ix: "At the center of the mind in Shelley's collective works are a denial of any self-evident truths that may serve as constructive first principles and a consequent indecision between contradictory desires for worldly perfection and an ideal postmortal eternity." Further, from pp. 471–72: "The radical indeterminacy of poems like *Alastor, Julian and Maddalo*, and the hymns of Pan and Apollo . . . is his frank admission that he has no assured basis on which to arrive at truth: everything presents two contradictory faces, both of which are equally defensible and equally untenable. . . . Even when, in poems like "Mont Blanc" and "The Sensitive Plant," he distinguishes between the two opposing faces of reality in terms of the senses and the imagination, and opts for the imaginative vision as the more believable, he remains honestly skeptical and acknowledges the purely speculative, or fideistic, nature of his choice, as the tentative endings of those poems suggest." I am rather more closely in accord with Harold Bloom's view of Shelley's skepticism, since he tends to speak of Shelley's poetry as a poetry of experience. From p. 91 of *The Ringers in the Tower: Studies in Romantic Tradition* (Chicago and London, 1971): "The deepest characteristic of Shelley's poetic mind is its skepti-

cism. Shelley's intellectual agnosticism was more fundamental than either his troubled materialism or his desperate idealism. Had the poet turned his doubt against all entities but his own poetry, while sparing that, he would have anticipated certain later developments in the history of literature, but his own work would have lost one of its most precious qualities, a unique sensitivity to its own limitations."

CHAPTER THREE

Transforming Nature: "Mont Blanc" and "Ode to the West Wind"

Through "Hymn to Intellectual Beauty" Shelley discovers that to grasp his own experience, he needs to fictionalize it. The poem converts the life of Percy Bysshe Shelley into the life of a narrator, who by the aid of a transforming image formulates the significance of his fluctuating responses to life. "Mont Blanc," Shelley's major version of the Wordsworthian poem of natural meditation, is kin to "Hymn to Intellectual Beauty": here, in order to grasp the significance of nature, the poet discovers he must fictionalize it. The achievement of "Mont Blanc" is the imagining of a poetic world which successfully stands as an interpretation of the world of nature. Of course, Wordsworth also interprets nature through his poetry; but I shall argue in this chapter that the Wordsworthian and Shelleyan modes of imaginative transformation exhibit important differences. A comparison of "Mont Blanc" with "Lines Composed a Few Miles Above

Tintern Abbey," the poem that serves as a model for "Mont
Blanc," [1] will clarify this point.

The poems begin with a difference which suggests an important
Shelleyan challenge of Wordsworth. "Tintern Abbey" starts
with a view of the Wye valley and moves inward to a meditation
upon its spiritual implications, but "Mont Blanc" begins in the
world of the mind with an abstract image, and only in section II
of the poem moves outward to a view of the ravine of Arve. [2] The
rationale for the Wordsworthian movement from the outside
world to the inside is his faith in "How exquisitely the individual
Mind . . . to the external World/ Is fitted . . . and how exquisitely
too . . . The external World is fitted to the Mind" (*The Recluse*,
Part I, Book I, 816–21). This fittingness bridging mind and nature makes smooth transitions from one to the other possible,
and indeed, inevitable; for if one begins with a natural prospect,
the resemblance of its forms to one's own thoughts will induce a
progress from observation to meditation.

In the Shelleyan feeling for experience, the gentle and gradated
movement that makes Wordsworthian transitions from nature to
mind possible is replaced by a sense of wild and uncontrolled
movement. It is this dizzying motion which destroys coherence.
The relation between mind and nature is unclear for Shelley not
because there possibly may be no relationship, but because the
connection is so intimate and fluxional as to preclude intel-
ligibility. This sense of things is derived from the British
Empirical view of cognition. As Shelley himself states the case, in
Speculations on Metaphysics,

> . . . thought can with difficulty visit the intricate and wind-
> ing chambers which it inhabits. It is like a river whose rapid
> and perpetual stream flows outwards;—like one in dread who
> speeds through the recesses of some haunted pile, and dares
> not look behind. The caverns of the mind are obscure, and
> shadowy; or pervaded with a lustre, beautifully bright in-
> deed, but shining not beyond their portals. If it were possible

to be where we have been, vitally and indeed—if, at the moment of our presence there, we could define the results of our experience,—if the passage from sensation to reflection—from a state of passive perception to voluntary contemplation, were not so dizzying and so tumultous, this attempt would be less difficult.

(VII, 64)

The first verse paragraph of "Mont Blanc" turns these observations into poetry, as the poem's speaker tries to construct an image that will explain the order of world and mind. His image pictures the mind as a vague and shadowy receptacle through which the river of the world forever flows, augmented by the tributary "feeble brook" (7) of human thought which rises from "secret springs" (4).[3] Although this image refers to incessant motion and to unremitting reverberation of sound and refraction of light, it should be emphasized that the image itself does not move. In itself it is a cognitive model, a general hypothesis, that proposes an explanation for the empirical phenomena of experience. From the start, then, "Mont Blanc" is fictional. Shelley proceeds not empirically and naturalistically, as does Wordsworth, but abstractly. For him, image is related to world-view: he needs a model of the cosmos before he can begin to grasp the meaning of his experience.

Such modelling potentially could order not only the universe, but the self; and indeed, the interactive aspects of Shelley's proposed model make clear that world-order and mind-order might be dual aspects of a dynamic unity. As we have seen in Chapter I, this is also the case for Hume. In his philosophy the dissolution of world-order inevitably is accompanied by the fragmenting of personal unity. When Hume tries to examine his own experience, to "enter most intimately into what I call *myself*,"[4] he never can perceive more than the incessant flow of his impressions. At any possible moment he will have "some particular perception or other, of heat or cold, light or shade, love or hatred, pain or pleasure. I never can catch *myself* at any time without a perception." Consequently, he can experience his personal identity only as "a bundle or collection of different perceptions, which succeed each other with an inconceivable rapidity, and are in perpetual flux and movement." And once the Humean perceiver is deprived of personal coherence, his world also bursts into fragments, also becomes a random "bundle or collection" rather than an organized whole. The case is the same for Shelley. In "Mont Blanc," as in "Hymn to Intellectual Beauty" and *Alastor*, the poet is mysterious to himself. The incessant movement that so plagues him is manifested both in his flowing perceptions of the world and in his fluctuating sense of self. Accordingly, gaining a grasp on his experience will imply the simultaneous acquisition of personal and world order.[5]

But the first world-image proposed in "Mont Blanc" proves inadequate to formulate experience. The abstraction of Shelley's image is an abstraction from nature: the mind is compared to a shadowy cavern or riverbed, and the world and human thought flow through it like a river. As this comparison is elaborated, the natural world by insensible degrees begins to move into the speaker's meditations. Human thought turns out to be like a "feeble brook . . . In the wild woods, among the mountains lone," surrounded by "waterfalls" and flowing toward a "vast river" (7–11). Finally, at the beginning of section II, he looks up and observes, "Thus thou, Ravine of Arve" (12)—for his abstraction merely has recapitulated the forms of the landscape before which he stands.[6] If in his image the mind is a receptacle and the universe of things is a river flowing through it, in turn, the poet sees before him a steep ravine through which the Arve races. And if his abstract universe of things flows by so swiftly that understanding it is impossible, so also this natural valley is "pervaded with . . . ceaseless motion,/ [is] the path of that unresting sound—/ Dizzy ravine!" (32–34). His model has failed to hold

steady because the elements of his imagery (rivers and their river-
beds) derive from nature and exhibit an irresistible tendency to
flow back into it.

But this reversion does not at all imply that his meditations can
find a stable confirmation in nature. In section II the poet's eye
scans the ravine, restlessly searching for meaning in what he sees;
but just as the mind's source is "secret springs" in his abstraction,
so the Arve comes down from a "secret throne" (17), and the
river seems to be a concealing appearance—it is "Power in likeness of the Arve" (16) rather than power itself. Similarly, the
torrent's great waterfall becomes a "veil" that "Robes some un-
sculptured image" (26–27), a sight that vaguely suggests but does
not reveal an underlying form. The poet's dilemma is that if his
model has been made in the likeness of nature, in turn, nature
seems to be a likeness of some other form hungered for by the
mind. In this sense, the strange result of his observation is that
nature itself also becomes a kind of abstraction—a clearer and
vaster picture than his own imagery, perhaps, but definitely not
the base and root of things.

So the searching poet turns from nature back to mind. This
time, instead of accepting the Lockean assumption that mind and
world are inextricably related in the act of perception, he hypothesizes that there can be "my own separate phantasy,/ My own,
my human mind," and set apart from it, "the clear universe of
things around" (36–40). Given this independence, the mind might
abandon the world for "the still cave of the witch Poesy," where
it could seek "among the shadows that pass by,/ Ghosts of all
things that are" (44–46).

This second proposed world-image is adapted from the passage
in Plato's *Republic* where Socrates tells his story about prisoners
in a cave who think they are perceiving reality, but actually see
only the shadows, thrown by firelight upon the cavern walls, of
artificial shapes carried on the heads of passing porters—reality at

the third remove, as it were.[7] Socrates suggests these people should emerge from the cavern into the natural sunlight. But it is clear why Shelley would like to visit such a cave: unlike both the eternally flowing world river of the Empirical image and the wildly racing Arve in nature, this place is "still." In this Platonic cave our perceptions are stabilized—if we see only "ghosts," at least we see them reasonably clearly.

In the end, however, ghosts cannot be adequate substitutes for reality. The poet eventually will have to leave his hypothetical cavern in search of the reality that the Platonic myth claims is outside. He imagines himself doing so, hovering on wings over "the clear universe of things around" in search of the real Arve; but instead of encountering the Platonic Form he can find only "thy darkness," in which, simply, "thou art there!" (40–48)—in the obscure confusion of unformulated experience. The Platonic world context, which in this poet's version suggests correspondences between ghostly poetic forms and real things, has failed to hold steady, just as the Empirical one did. In the contemplated Platonic searching for formal resemblances one would be compelled to move around an indefinitely repeating cycle between cave and clear universe, racing in pursuit of correspondences that never really become evident.

In retrospect, we can see that sections I and II of "Mont Blanc," as a whole, have enacted a rather similar cycling. The poet has begun with one world image that failed to hold stable, has given it up to become absorbed in a dizzily moving natural landscape that remained puzzling, and finally has retreated to yet another cosmic image which also fails to halt the world's movement. At the end of all this experience the poet scarcely knows more than he did at the beginning, and he is left with his original problem: the need somehow to transcend the incessant motion of experience in order to discover a stable world context. With Hume, he has found human experience to be "a bundle or collection of

different perceptions, which succeed each other with an inconceivable rapidity, and are in perpetual flux and movement"; and
neither the surrender to the flow of phenomena nor the attempt to
arrest that flow by the creation of clear imagery has yielded an
authentic solution to his problem of severe disorientation.

But the beginning of section III suddenly witnesses a break in
the dizzying round. The poet exclaims, "I look on high;/ Has
some unknown omnipotence unfurled/ The veil of life and
death? . . . Far, far above, piercing the infinite sky,/ Mont Blanc
appears" (52–61). Shelley's letter of July 22, 1816, to Peacock,
which describes his visit to Mont Blanc, casts light on this passage; he says that during his party's approach to the Alps, "Mont
Blanc was before us but was covered with cloud, & its base
furrowed with dreadful gaps was seen alone. Pinnacles of snow,
intolerably bright, part of the chain connected with Mont Blanc
shone thro the clouds at intervals on high. I never knew I never
imagined what mountains were before. The immensity of these
aerial summits excited, when they suddenly burst upon the sight,
a sentiment of extatic wonder, not unallied to madness—And
remember this was all one scene. It all pressed home to our regard
& to our imagination." [8] The letter reveals a fascination with
how high mountains can "suddenly burst upon the sight" when
winds dispel their cloud cover. Clearly, this is what has happened
as section III of "Mont Blanc" begins. As Shelley says in his
letter, such a view formed "one scene. It all pressed home to our
regard & to our imagination." In other words, an immense vista
appears under the aspect of unity, which is produced precisely by
its *sudden exposure*.

The achievement of this visionary moment in "Mont Blanc"
can be compared usefully to the equivalent moment in "Tintern
Abbey." Whereas Shelley's vision is an abrupt revelation, an
insight utterly discontinuous with the previous flow of his meditations, Wordsworth approaches vision by methods of smooth

transition and harmony.[9] His initial description of the landscape suggests this; for the valley's cliffs "connect/ The landscape with the quiet of the sky," the orchard-tufts "Are clad in one green hue, and lose themselves/ 'Mid groves and copses," and the farmhouses are "Green to the very door." As the landscape reveals gradual transitions between the world of nature and the world of man, so the poet's visionary moment is the climax of a gradual modulation from the world of body to the world of spirit. He experiences "that serene and blessed mood,/ In which the affections gently lead us on" into a peaceful trancelike state wherein "the motion of our human blood/ Almost suspended, we are laid asleep/ In body." Then this organic tranquillity is transposed into a state of spiritual grace, so that with "an eye made quiet by the power/ Of harmony, and the deep power of joy,/ We see into the life of things." In "Tintern Abbey" the fitting relationship between body and mind, sight and insight, flows smoothly; similarly, the relationship perceived between nature and God becomes a harmonious transition. In his vision the poet senses "A motion and a spirit, that impels/ All thinking things, all objects of all thought,/ And rolls through all things."

Like the gently murmuring Wye that exemplifies the mode of motion in "Tintern Abbey," Wordsworth's God is a presence that emerges harmoniously within natural forms. But what Shelley sees in the summit of Mont Blanc is an absolute discontinuity in nature, which is the terrible counterpart of the disjunctive flash of his vision. The Arve ravine is a place of life, filled with sound, color, living forms, and incessant motion; but the summit of Mont Blanc is its deathly reverse. Here rivers of water become the "frozen floods" of glaciers (64), and the world's spectrum of colors is absorbed into the absolute of white. Most important, the reverberating voices of the wildly moving Arve and its living ravine are countered by the motionless quiet of Mont Blanc— "still, snowy, and serene" (61). Given this vision, the poet's foremost problem is the discovery of some kind of connection between these vastly different parts of the world. The sense that all things are related, which comes naturally to Wordsworth, becomes an achievement for Shelley. Where Wordsworth's mode of poetic vision can be transitional—a smooth and fitting passage from nature to mind—Shelley's will have to be transformational. Somehow, the poet of "Mont Blanc" must convert a nature seemingly without human significance into a humanly relevant vision.[10]

Of course, it is true that in section IV of the poem the poet's glance sweeps down from the peak to the ravine, discovering a kind of connectedness in things through the chain of cause and effect in nature. From this perspective he sees that the mountain presides over an eternal natural cycle: snow, which is precipitated on the peak, becomes the ice of the glaciers, which in turn becomes the water of the Arve, which flows to the sea and is evaporated, becoming the clouds that drop snow on Mont Blanc to begin the entire process again. But if natural causality provides some sort of connection, the point is that it is not the kind that can satisfy the poet's human cravings. As with the riverlike flow of impressions through the ravinelike human mind of section I, the movements involved in this natural cycle have no meaning for the observer. He is a living creature, but nature dispenses life (in the valley) and death (on the mountain) quite differently. Its purpose, if it can be said to have one, is merely the perpetuation of its own cyclical motion.

But this is only one of the implications of the poet's vision, and actually, it turns out to be a subordinate one. If the glimpse of Mont Blanc's deathly ice fields has illustrated the meaninglessness of merely natural motion just as did the meditations of section II, the poet's mode of vision itself has not shared in that motion. Because of its very brevity, his flash of insight cannot move: in the words of Shelley's letter, Mont Blanc has "suddenly burst upon the sight," revealed in the frozen way a photograph reveals things rather than as a motion picture does. This makes it possible for the immense arrested panorama to become a stable context, organized around the center of the mountain peak. In other words, because of the singular way in which it has appeared, the poet can construe Mont Blanc as a transforming image.

Indeed, the Empirical model of cognition dominating section I of the poem is not inconsistent with this novel development, even though it does not anticipate it. There the river of our impressions flows by incessantly, just as here the causes and effects involved in Mont Blanc's hydrological cycle convert snow to ice to water to vapor incessantly. If it is impossible to perceive the power that connects one impression to the next in the mind, it is also impossible to see how cause links to effect in the natural world. This was Hume's revolutionary insight, discovered by Shelley in the original and also in Godwin's and Drummond's adaptations; and what it meant was that in effect, there seems to be a kind of ontological gap between every impression and the one that follows it, and between every natural cause and its succeeding effect. As Shelley explains it, in a fragment he titled *On Polytheism*: "All we know of cause is that one event, or to speak more correctly, one sensation follows another attended with a conviction derived from experience that these sensations will hereafter be similarly connected. This habitual conviction is that to which we appeal when we say that one thing is the cause of another, or has the power of producing certain effects" (VII, 151). For Shelley, who believes that "nothing exists but as it is perceived," there can be no categorical differences between external "causes" and internal "impressions." Anything we are aware of can be categorized as a perception, and so the flow of cause and effect and the flow of impressions are interchangeable expressions designating the same phenomenon ("one event, or to speak more correctly, one sensation"). In this passage Shelley correctly ex-

pounds the Humean argument that this flow of experienced
phenomena gains its authority from our "habitual conviction":
because we have seen things joined in a certain serial order many
times in the past, we expect them to come in the same succession
in the future. In other words, it is human habit, not God, or the
relations of "things in themselves," that accounts for the particular ordering of our perceptions.

If this is so, then it is possible for a transforming image to enter
any of the innumerable lacunae between one of our habitual
impressions and the next, and by suddenly supplying a new
context for our perceptual field, to reorder the entire serial flow of
our experience. In his letter to Peacock, Shelley exclaims, "I
never knew I never imagined what mountains were before." This
does not mean that the poet never has seen mountains, it means
that he never has seen them *in this way.* As Shelley says in the
Defence of Poetry:

> . . . poetry defeats the curse which binds us to be subjected to
> the accident of surrounding impressions. . . . It makes us
> the inhabitants of a world to which the familiar world is a
> chaos. It reproduces the common Universe of which we are
> portions and percipients, and it purges from our inward sight
> the film of familiarity which obscures from us the wonder
> of our being. It compels us to feel that which we perceive,
> and to imagine that which we know. It creates anew the
> universe, after it has been annihilated in our minds by the
> recurrence of impressions blunted by reiteration.
>
> (VII, 137)

But this renewal of the universe is not a frequent phenomenon,
nor one that can be willed. If it were, it would be a habitual
response, which means that it would lose its cardinal value of
novelty. So "A man cannot say, 'I will compose poetry.' The
greatest poet even cannot say it" (VII, 135).

However, the speaker of "Mont Blanc" has been trying to say

something of the sort in sections I and II of the poem. He has summoned the hackneyed images of the Empirical river of impressions and the Platonic cave of false forms in order to conceptualize his experience in the ravine of Arve, but these conscious attempts have not served. Then, in section III, Mont Blanc appears from behind the clouds, an event over which he has no control. Similarly, his perception of this event exceeds the powers of will. As in the "Hymn to Intellectual Beauty," where the child's willful pursuit of ghosts suddenly is transformed by the unwilled descent of Beauty, this speaker's deliberate effort to understand the operations of his own mind suddenly is transformed by an unwilled expansion of his powers of insight. And as in the "Hymn," he reverences this mysterious visitation, feeling it to be the presence of "some unknown omnipotence" (53) under which his "very spirit fails/ Driven like a homeless cloud from steep to steep/ That vanishes among the viewless gales!" (57–59). The conscious self is dispelled like the clouds that blow away from Mont Blanc, leaving something different, and far more sublime, exposed there. Shelley speaks of this new presence in terms of expansion, of circles that broaden their scope as the concentric ripples in a pond radiate from an object dropped in the water. He marvels, "do I lie/ In dream, and does the mightier world of sleep/ Spread far around and inaccessibly/ Its circles?" (54–57). As in the *Defence of Poetry*, here "Poetry enlarges the circumference of the imagination" (VII, 118) by revealing powers within the speaker that exceed his center of self. In section II he willfully cherished "my own separate phantasy,/ My own, my human mind" (36–37); here he has died to his own selfhood and been reborn in his aspect of divinity.

But in "Mont Blanc," divinity does not speak; it merely manifests itself. Although the poet says that Mont Blanc has a "voice" that "repeal[s]/ Large codes of fraud and woe," and that its attendant wilderness has a "mysterious tongue" (76–80), in fact, the only speech we hear in this poem is the speech of the poet. He *interprets* what he has seen, thereby supplying a voice for the mountain, which in itself remains "Still, snowy, and serene" (61). The conspicuous silence of the mountain and the speech of its poet suggest an important property of the transforming image. Such images are cryptic; they do not explain themselves, they merely appear. Their manifestation points toward a mysterious divinity in nature and in human beings; but if Mont Blanc itself remains impenetrable in this poem, it is equally true that the poet's own divinity remains a thing apart from "my own, my human mind" (37). It is the role of that human mind to witness the appearance of divinity and then articulate the meaning of the image.[11]

His first reaction is a kind of sublime dismay, for he sees clearly that the Wordsworthian intimation of a loving presence dwelling within nature is but a half truth. Although the Arve "Rolls its loud waters to the ocean waves,/ Breathes its swift vapours to the circling air," thus becoming the living "breath and blood of distant lands" (124–26), very much as the Wye flows through Wordsworth's poem and helps him sense "A motion and a spirit, that impels/ All thinking things, all objects of all thought,/ And rolls through all things," it is also true that the ice field of Mont Blanc, the source of the Arve's waters, is a place of death. The tumult of the river's icy waters above now also suggests the sacred/demonic world of "Kubla Khan"; the Arve issues "from those secret chasms in tumult welling" (122), as in Coleridge's poem, the Alph's waters come "from this chasm, with ceaseless turmoil seething."[12]

The world, it seems, is vaster than the poet could have imagined: the world of nature, and also the world of himself, which must rise to meet the sublimity presented to him. He instinctively moves to possess nature in the embrace of his feeling because he sees the world as splendid but terrible and senses that someone must care for it. No God has spoken for the world through his transforming vision; it follows that he himself must speak. The suddenly enlarged perception of the poet, which has allowed him to sense the universe as a whole, is rivalled by his suddenly enlarged spiritual scope. He becomes great enough to embrace the vast panorama he sees. As the *Defence* puts it, he is compelled to "feel that which [he] perceives, and to imagine that which [he] knows" (VII, 137).

So he speaks to the world in the language of love, addressing it as a "Thou" rather than an "it" (lines 12, 13, 19, 20, 25, 30, 32, 33, 34, 42, 43, 46, 48, 80, 141, 142).[13] Finally his feeling becomes so large that it can embrace even death and find value there, too. He sees the deadly glaciers moving down the valley, overthrowing

> The limits of the dead and living world,
> Never to be reclaimed. The dwelling-place
> Of insects, beasts, and birds becomes its spoil;
> Their food and their retreat forever gone,
> So much of life and joy is lost. The race
> Of man flies far in dread; his work and dwelling
> Vanish, like smoke before the tempest's stream,
> And their place is not known.
>
> (113–20)

Here, eloquence redeems the waste of death. "So much of life and joy is lost." We are moved not to despair but to an even greater love of life because by the very expression of its loss, we poignantly realize its value. If the poet fails to redeem nature through this kind of feeling, the result will be "awful doubt" (75), the discovery of the meaninglessness of merely natural forms. But the visionary lover of nature himself projects meaning into the universe by acts so immense in scope that he transcends the parts of the world and embraces the whole, producing a sublime "faith so mild,/ So solemn, so serene" (77–78) that it resembles the quiet

summit of Mont Blanc itself, or the motionless moment of poetic
vision.

It is to that mountain summit that the poet's vision reverts in
section V, to the still center of the moving world which is also the
image of his own divinely still center.[14] Now we can see that by
talking to the mountain he has found a way of talking to his own
visionary self, and in loving nature, he has found a way to love his
own conscious self. The resolution of the poem is similar to the
resolution of the "Hymn to Intellectual Beauty," where the
speaker also was seen to be addressing the divine aspect of himself, through the indirection of poetic discourse. In the end,
although the poem is both religious and philosophical, it expresses
neither a religion nor a philosophy, but a personal vision. By
creating a poetic fiction, this speaker has been able to grasp the
meaning of his own experience. As a transforming image the
mountain has served to formulate this poet's feelings; but if it was
perceived by another, it might release a quite different poem. As
Shelley remarks in his letter to Peacock, "Do you who assert the
supremacy of Ahriman imagine him throned among these desolat-
ing snows, among these palaces of death & frost, sculptured in
this their terrible magnificence by the unsparing hand of necessity,
& that he casts around him as the first essays of his final usurpa-
tion avalanches, torrents, rocks & thunders—and above all, these
deadly glaciers at once the proofs & the symbols of his reign—"
(I, 499). Here is an opposing imagination of the world, in which
Mont Blanc becomes the transforming image of tyranny rather
than of Shelleyan imaginative love. Remarkably, either of these
visions fits all the observed facts of nature equally well.[15]

This astounding range in the imaginative possibilities helps
emphasize what nature at last becomes for the poet in "Mont
Blanc." In redeeming nature through the embrace of his feeling,
what he finally does is make nature a mirror in which he can see
himself. His personal involvement transforms the natural universe

into a poetic universe. As with the "Hymn to Intellectual Beauty," this poetry embodies not a glimpse of transcendental truth, but a transformational fiction—a way of indirectly knowing oneself.[16]

At the beginning of his poem the poet speculated that the "source of human thought" was a "feeble brook" that made only a minor contribution to the riverlike "everlasting universe of things"; the poem's expression has demonstrated that just the opposite is true. The universe of things actually is a function of human vision—as a person is, so will his world be. In themselves, nature's cycles of cause and effect show no ontological linkage, as Hume suggests; but the language of the poet provides a visionary unity for nature by projecting the global form of the poet's personality into it. In turn, nature allows the poet to create his own personal unity by articulating the meaning of the images he perceives. The relationship of mind and nature at last envisioned in "Mont Blanc" is neither Empirical nor Platonic; for unlike the Empirical model, it is not merely a serial relationship, and unlike the Platonic model, it is not dualistic. Rather, the relationship is an expressive unity—global in its conception, serial in its articulation. The world and the self become dual functions of the poet's speech.[17] In speaking the poem he expresses a world, so that his composition becomes a cosmos, a fictional analogue of the actual world. His imagery transforms nature into a personal poetry: Mont Blanc as *Ding an sich* remains an unknown quantity, but Mont Blanc as an image becomes the organizing center of his visionary world.

In "Tintern Abbey" Wordsworth refers to "all the mighty world/ Of eye and ear,—both what they half create,/ And what perceive," thus suggesting a blending or transitional model for the relationship between man and nature. If "Mont Blanc" also suggests some basis for the relationship between man and nature, and in that sense makes a poetic affirmation similar to that of "Tintern Abbey," nevertheless it must be emphasized that Shelley's view is far more radical than Wordsworth's. The Shelleyan poet does more than "half create," since what is there to "perceive" can be interpreted in an indefinitely large number of ways. As the focus of perception in Shelley's poem, Mont Blanc appropriately exemplifies this Shelleyan sense of things: in itself white and still, it awaits the seeing and saying of the poet. Poets bring images out of blankness, speech out of silence, and in so doing they create a world we can know. But "Mont Blanc" only skeptically affirms this process of world-creation. Because the poet realizes that each of us expresses himself through nature, he does not force his particular vision upon us as a transcendental apprehension of Truth. The poem ends with the freedom of a question addressed to the enigmatic mountain:

> And what were thou, and earth, and stars, and sea,
> If to the human mind's imaginings
> Silence and solitude were vacancy?
>
> (142–44)

Mont Blanc's silence and solitude are not vacancy to the mind's imaginings, but neither can they be transcendentally formulated: out of these lacunae may spring an immensely wide range of personal expressions.

Like "Mont Blanc," "Ode to the West Wind" turns upon the poet's perception that the world of nature and the world of poetry are separate and can be related only through ever-renewed acts of poetic expression. Just as the speaker of "Mont Blanc" created a fictional cosmos that enabled him to grasp the meaning of his own experience, so the speaker of the "Ode" is moved to make sense of the natural world precisely because its processes threaten to render his life meaningless. The wind in this poem is both "Destroyer and Preserver" (13)[18]—destroyer of the autumn world, prophet and preserver of the coming spring. As with the hydrological cycle of "Mont Blanc," which perpetuates itself but is indifferent to the continuation of human life and value, the yearly cycle of this ode suggests the immortality of nature at the same time that it implies the mortality of individual human beings. In this sense, the West Wind refers to the natural forces that eventually will bring the poet's own death. Thus, the enterprise of the "Ode" is to "strive . . . with thee in prayer in my sore need" (51–52), to oppose the wind rather than giving in to it, in the hope of creating a world of enduring human value that somehow might offset the destruction inherent in the natural order.

As with the poems discussed earlier in this volume, that hoped-for realm of enduring value may seem to Shelley's readers to be transcendental. For like the "unseen Power" of Beauty in "Hymn to Intellectual Beauty" and the "Power" that "dwells apart" hidden in Mont Blanc, the West Wind is an "unseen" deity that nevertheless is "moving everywhere" (2, 13)—an invisible force which causes all the world's visible motion. Since power seems to originate beyond the world of appearance in these poems, their procedure might be to deploy Beauty, Mont Blanc, and the West Wind as symbols for a power that the poet sees as actually existing in a transcendental world. Shelley then could suggest that the order of mind might be related to the real order of this transcendental realm, a connection which would render the natural order of human life meaningful. But in fact, this is not the procedure of "Hymn to Intellectual Beauty" or "Mont Blanc." That it also is not the procedure of "Ode to the West Wind" can be inferred in the ode's stance toward nature: it creates a relationship between the human and natural orders not by congruence, but by an insistent competition.

In the first three sections of the "Ode," the poet is moved to speech by the realization of his own powerlessness. He sees that the West Wind completely dominates the sky, the surface of earth, and the places under the sea—in effect, that it controls the entire world. This cosmic mastery by the wind seems to leave no room for the assertion of human powers. However, the grammar of these first sections subtly suggests that this might not be the case. This poet's way of speech places actual power at the end of his periods, which when arrived at, defranchise the very obvious powers of the wind extensively described in the body of each sentence. The first section of the poem is one very long period, and the second and third each are divided into only two sentences. All three sections conclude with the injunction "O, hear!" (14, 28, 42), and in each case, this is the verb that governs the entire section. Apparently, the poet's command that his plea be heard has such strength as to subordinate the very movements of the West Wind.[19]

But how can this be so? Within the world of the poem, the necessary power is conferred by the speaker's grasp of a transforming image. In the fifth section he sees himself as the wind's lyre (57), an aeolian harp ravaged by the wind's strength, bursting forth into "a deep, autumnal tone,/ Sweet though in sadness" (60–61). His poetic voice has become a human transformation of the wind's breath, a conversion of the wind's force into the powerfully moving "incantation of this verse" (65). The *Defence of Poetry* uses a similar image to explain the power of imagination:

> Man is an instrument over which a series of external and internal impressions are driven, like the alternations of an ever-changing wind over an aeolian lyre, which move it by their motion to ever-changing melody. But there is a principle within the human being . . . which acts otherwise than in the lyre, and produces not melody alone, but harmony, by an internal adjustment of the sounds or motions thus excited to the impressions which excite them. It is as if the lyre could accommodate its chords to the motions of that which strikes them, in a determined proportion of sound; even as the musician can accommodate his voice to the sound of the lyre.
> (VII, 109–10)

The music of this lyre is a transformation, a conversion of the wind's sound into a human "melody," and beyond that, into a complex "harmony" that becomes a context enfolding the melody, a world of sound in which it sings its solo. The wind passes through the human mind and emerges as a poem.

Thus, the "Ode to the West Wind" is transformational, not transcendental. It is a poem that changes the world of nature into a human world, the voice of the West Wind into the poet's voice. As in "Mont Blanc," the poet's speech appropriates the world—this is why he can be more powerful than the West Wind. The difference between the two poems is that speech now has been intensified into song; Shelley has entered fully into the lyric mode, and, in his major poetry, will practice it for the rest of his career.

From this transformational perspective we can see the poem is a fiction that allows the poet to address the hidden divinity in himself, just as the poet of "Hymn to Intellectual Beauty" and of "Mont Blanc" seemed to be addressing an external divinity but at last could be seen to be worshipping his own visionary powers. The natural wind cannot really listen to this ode; that is only within the power of the poet himself. When he implores the West Wind, "O hear!," actually he is commanding himself to rise to the prayerful strife of poetry, which overcomes nature by transforming it. Below Shelley's manuscript draft of the poem he triumphantly inscribed a line in Greek from Euripides: "By virtue I, a mortal, vanquish thee, a mighty god." [20]

The world of enduring human value he affirms by his vanquishing of the natural god is the world of culture, that "great poem which all poets . . . have built up since the beginning of the world" extolled in the *Defence*. Insofar as he remains a part of nature, the poet himself someday must meet the death he foresees; but his poetic creations will live on after him, preserved in the ongoing life of human culture. His poem shows us how the "sparks" (67) of his words will be blown into the minds of yet unborn generations, where they will create new conflagrations. But this vision of his poetic immortality is not something that exists objectively, beyond the poem. As in "Ozymandias," where the sculptor's image lives only through the imaginative perceptions of his artistic descendants, the traveller in the antique land and the writer of the sonnet, so also, the life of the "Ode" must be recreated continually in the kindling perceptions of its new readers, generation after generation. When the poet's words cease to spark us, they will become as mortal as his natural self. The prayerful strife of poetry is not completed by the speaker of "Ode to the West Wind"; it remains always as a new challenge to the living.

Therefore, the poem ends not with the driving assertiveness of the wind, but with the skeptical freedom of a question that suggests the boundaries of poems and poetic worlds: "O Wind,/ If Winter comes, can Spring be far behind?" (69–70). Certainly not, in the order of nature. But for his human purposes this speaker has transformed nature's wind into a fictional presence— an image, an analogy of his own divinity. It is quite possible that the analogy will not hold in all contexts. The incantatory emotion that drives us on within the confines of the poem may, at any point outside those barriers, be dispersed. In the end, the commitment to faith, hope, the transformation of human life, is our own choice; and the poet can provide only a vision of power, he cannot literally supply power to his listeners. As with "Mont Blanc," which also ends in a question, the poet has swept us up in his emotion but in the end does not try to force his vision upon us. His last act is to remind us of our freedom.

NOTES

1   For a compact account of Wordsworth's influence on *Alastor*, the "Hymn to Intellectual Beauty," and "Mont Blanc," see Harold Bloom, *The Visionary Company: A Reading of English Romantic Poetry*, revised and enlarged edition (Ithaca, N.Y., 1971), pp. 285–96. For Bloom's discussion of the relationship between "Tintern Abbey" and "Mont Blanc," see *Shelley's Mythmaking* (New Haven, Conn., 1959), p. 20.

2. Judith Chernaik, *The Lyrics of Shelley* (Cleveland and London, 1972), p. 29.

3. The text of "Mont Blanc" referred to in this chapter is from Chernaik, *The Lyrics of Shelley*. For a comparison of this edition with the fair copy of "Mont Blanc" made by Shelley, which was discovered in the Scrope Davies find, see Judith Chernaik and Timothy Burnett, "The Byron and Shelley Notebooks in the Scrope Davies Find," *RES* new series, vol. xxxix, no. 113 (Feb., 1978), pp. 36–49.

Shelley's image of the world-river and the secret springs of human thought recapitulates the Empirical view of experience as a phenomenal flow and is not really very original. Although the Empirical philosophers were more inclined to describe the flow of experience as a "train" of ideas or impressions, in Godwin Shelley would have seen it referred to as "the unity of uninterrupted succession, the perennial flow as of a stream" (*An Enquiry Concerning Political Justice*, 1793, Book IV, chapter IX); and he would have read about "the secret spring of this unlooked-for event" (Book IV, chapter VII). In Hume he could have read a now famous passage announcing the philosopher's intention to "discover, at least in some degree, the secret springs and principles, by which the human mind is activated in its operations" (*An Enquiry Concerning Human Understanding*, 1758, section I).

However, this Empirical "spring" often carries mechanical rather than natural associations. For example, consider this passage from Volume Five, chapter Six of *Tristram Shandy*: "Though in one sense, our family was certainly a single machine, as it consisted of a few wheels; yet there was this much to be said for it, that these wheels were set in motion by so many different springs, and acted one upon the other from such a variety of strange principles and impulses.—that though it was a simple machine, it had all the honour and advantages of a complex one.—"

4. See text, pp. 11–12.

5. For a reading of "Mont Blanc" which ignores Shelley's Empirical antecedents in order to convert his quest for order into a Derridan search for origins, see Leslie Brisman, *Romantic Origins* (Ithaca and London, 1978), pp. 377–86. Although I believe the historical context of Shelley's Empirical interests provides a better basis for discussion of "Mont Blanc" than does Derrida's theory of writing and poetry, I agree with Brisman that the voice which speaks in the poem must "be recognized as a fiction" (p. 383).

6. For a detailed treatment of this aspect of the poem, see Earl R. Wasserman, *Shelley: A Critical Reading* (Baltimore, 1971), pp. 224–27.

7. James A. Notopoulos considers the myth of the cave in the *Republic* to be the source of Shelley's imagery. See *The Platonism of Shelley* (Durham, N.C., 1949), p. 208. For other accounts of the influence of Plato's myth on "Mont Blanc," see I. J. Kapstein, "The Meaning of Shelley's

'Mont Blanc,'" *PMLA* 62, no. 4, part I (Dec., 1947), pp. 1046–60, and especially, p. 1052; and Wasserman, *Shelley*, p. 227.

8. *The Letters of Percy Bysshe Shelley*, ed. Frederick L. Jones, 2 vols. (Oxford, 1964), I, p. 497. All references to Shelley's letters are based on this edition and will be noted by volume and page number in the text.

9. See text, pp. 12–16 for a discussion of the abruptness of visionary experience in Shelley.

10. Shelley's opposition to the merely natural is emphasized in Bloom's readings. See *The Visionary Company*, p. 293: "The mountain and its ravine testify to Shelley of the difficulties inherent in natural theology, in our seeking to find the wisdom of God in the creation."

11. Kenneth Neil Cameron, in *Shelley: The Golden Years* (Cambridge, Mass., 1974), discusses an interesting usage in the poem that, I think, points toward this gap between imagery and articulation. The word he comments on is in this passage:

> Power dwells apart in its tranquillity
> Remote, serene, and inaccessible:
> And *this*, the naked countenance of earth,
> On which I gaze, even these primeval mountains
> Teach the adverting mind.
>
> (96–100)

Cameron remarks: "The 'adverting mind' is apparently an echo from Godwin's chapter 'Of the Mechanism of the Human Mind' in *Political Justice*. 'Consciousness is a sort of supplementary reflection, by which the mind not only has the thought, but adverts to its own situation, and observes that it has it. Consciousness therefore, however nice the distinction, seems to be a second thought.'"

12. For a concise account of the relationship between "Kubla Khan" and "Mont Blanc," see Bloom, *The Visionary Company*, pp. 293–96.

13. Bloom grounds Shelley's "Thou's" in a mythmaking procedure that is illuminated through reference to the works of Martin Buber. See *Shelley's Mythmaking*, and especially, chapter I, "The Mythopoeic Mode."

14. When I wrote this passage I did not intentionally evoke Eliot; but the wording seems to be appropriate, and it calls attention to an area of agreement between two very different poets.

15. This feature of "Mont Blanc" and Shelley's letter to Peacock is reminiscent of Blake's *Songs of Innocence and Experience*. There, too, contrary world visions are based on the same facts.

16. In his valuable reading of "Mont Blanc," Wasserman extensively discusses the role of stillness and silence in the poem, but he finds that they have a transcendental reference: the dizzying motion and sound of the phenomenal world is occasioned by a quiet, motionless Power that is a paradoxically uncausing causality, a force from another world that

accounts for the phenomena of ours. As he sums it up: "Meaning lies in the mind's visionary apprehension of a single eternal, immutable, and amoral Power which lies behind the seemingly absurd mutability and recurrent emptiness, and of whose necessary laws the activities of the world are a manifestation. . . . Our mutable and deficient world makes sense and can be understood only if we can bring into it our extraordinary knowledge of the transcendent Power which is not mutable or discontinuous and from which all that is partial and deficient derives" (*Shelley*, pp. 237–38). On the contrary, I argue that the "Power" in "Mont Blanc" is, as Shelley says, something that "dwells apart in its tranquillity/ Remote, serene, and inaccessible" (96–97). The poet honors the unfathomable mysteries hidden in himself and the world, but what he sees in the poem is what in fact he *can* perceive—nature, transformed into a poetic form that manifests his personality.

17. See Susan Hawk Brisman, " 'Unsaying His High Language': The Problem of Voice in Prometheus Unbound," *SIR* 16, no. 1 (Winter 1977), pp. 51–86. On p. 58 Brisman calls attention to this passage of *Prometheus Unbound*: "[Prometheus] gave man speech, and speech created thought,/ Which is the measure of the universe" (II, iv., 72–73). She remarks, "Promethean utterance strives to bring word and world into being simultaneously, and to make their single presence the ground of all signification." I would add that in this passage speech also "created thought," so that expression brings into being not only the perceived world but also the speaker's self. The radically creative role of expression noted by Brisman in this article is closely related to the radically creative role of metaphor in John W. Wright's *Shelley's Myth of Metaphor* (Athens, Ga., 1970); and in this connection, both critics conduct discussions of language theory from the late 17th through early 19th centuries as a background to Shelley. Although these critics use very different vocabularies, they seem to me to be substantially in agreement. For my discussion of Wright, see text, pp. 4–5.

18. The text of "Ode to the West Wind" referred to in this chapter is from Chernaik, *The Lyrics of Shelley*.

19. Here the poem's grammar creates suggestions similar to those implied by the grammar of lines 84 through 97 of "Mont Blanc." The first twelve of these fourteen lines from "Mont Blanc" are a single sentence, an immense catalogue of all things in the world, considered under the aspect of life's incessant motion. The sentence closes with a summary of the catalogue: "All things that move and breathe with toil and sound/ Are born and die; revolve, subside and swell." The remarkable thing about this huge and bustling sentence is that for its manifold subjects there is no dominating verb; so that the tremendous motion takes place in a vacuum, as it were. The required verb shows up in the

following clause, and it supplies the sentence's action not through a mode of motion but by the paradoxical notion of uncausing causality: "Power dwells apart in its tranquillity/ Remote, serene, and inaccessible." Both this passage and the one from "Ode to the West Wind" enact the grammar of an indirect power transaction. This quality of indirection is related to the transformational relationship of the Shelleyan poet and his world. Indirection is more fully discussed in the chapter on *Prometheus Unbound*. chapter on *Prometheus Unbound*.

20. Quoted and translated in Neville Rogers, *Shelley at Work: A Critical Inquiry* (Oxford, 1956), p. 18. Also quoted in Richard Holmes, *Shelley: The Pursuit* (New York, 1975), p. 547. Holmes's and Rogers's translations differ slightly. Holmes has it, "By virtuous power, I, a mortal, vanquish thee a mighty god."

CHAPTER FOUR

The World Transformed:
Prometheus Unbound

In "Ode to the West Wind," Shelley sketches a relationship between man and nature that depends upon a transformational lyricism: the wind enters the singer's mind and emerges as a poem. This scheme is elaborated immensely in *Prometheus Unbound*, which shows lyricism to be the force that creates the civilized world. That is, songs transform the world of nature into the world of culture. Shelley's subtitle for *Prometheus Unbound*, "A Lyrical Drama," suggests that he was aware of the lyrical law governing his play. As his characters sing, so they will see.[1] The expression of their essential beings, delivered in the lyrical moment, will create the worlds that they then must inhabit. Thus, the world of *Prometheus Unbound* is not a transcendental world but a transformational one; its appearances are the indirect self-images that its characters have created through their own songs. To be free in such a world, one must understand transformation, so that changes can be willed rather than simply seeming to happen.

In her Notes on *Prometheus Unbound* Mary Shelley expressed her understanding of Shelley's views on moral change. She said Shelley "believed that mankind had only to will that there should be no evil, and there would be none," a statement not incorrect but certainly misleading. The central concern of *Prometheus Unbound* is the very process of willing change, which is shown to be complex, and above all, not straightforward. *Prometheus Unbound* suggests that just as poems are the indirect embodiment of their makers, the moral worlds perceived by persons are the indirect manifestations of themselves. The problem involved in willing change is therefore a problem of indirection. As the *Defence* says of poetry, "A man cannot say, 'I will compose poetry.' The greatest poet even cannot say it" (VII, 135). Similarly, a person cannot say "I will change myself," and simply be changed, as Mary Shelley's statement seems to suggest. Moral change, like poetry, is an imaginative process—a way of apprehending the world in inspired moments, which opens the way to a transformed global view.

But the moment of vision does not automatically bring change. Since the images involved in Shelleyan visionary experience are silent, they must be given a voice by he who witnesses them. As in "Mont Blanc," the transforming images must be interpreted—and that very act of interpretation then will establish a new grounding, or unity, for the speaker's personality. This mute property of Shelleyan imagery allows scope for the moral will in *Prometheus Unbound*, just as after visionary experience it allowed scope for the voluntary response of the poet in "Mont Blanc." In itself one's vision may be beyond one's control, but one's reaction to the experience, one's articulation of it, largely is within the realm of willed responses.

Through the experience of Prometheus and Asia, the play

shows two fundamental modes of interpreting transformational imagery. The mode of Prometheus, in the first Act, is the mode of restraint. He is presented with various imageries—the phantasm of Jupiter, the historical panoramas created by the Furies, the visions of hope brought by the Chorus of Spirits—and his reaction is to resist merging with these imageries, to force himself to stand back and decide what to make of them. Prometheus needs to behave in this restrained way precisely because his perceived world is the consequence of a prior act of tremendous self-indulgence. In cursing Jupiter he gave way to unrestrained anger, becoming, as he himself says in an echo of Milton's Samson, "eyeless in hate" (I, 9).[2] His lyric of execration has welled out uncontrolled and unexamined, so that unawares, he has created a poetic world of destruction. For him, the naive lyricism of hatred must be replaced by a world of much greater poetic and moral sophistication—he must understand what he is saying and take more care in formulating his statements. But if lyric restraint is necessary for Prometheus, the complimentary quality of lyrical surrender is required of Asia. Her experience in Act II begins with mysterious and evocative dream images that draw her out, demanding interpretation. Her heroism therefore becomes the heroism of surrender as she follows out her imagery, wherever it may lead, to discover its meaning for herself.

That Demogorgon introduces a necessitarian element into the drama in no way contradicts the claims I have been making for the extreme moral and poetic freedoms of *Prometheus Unbound*. Although Demogorgon presides over an inexorable chain of cause and effect, his "mighty law" (II, ii, 43) is not one law, and it is not the real law of an objective universe. Demogorgon himself is "Ungazed upon and shapeless," and claims that he cannot be oracular because "a voice/ Is wanting, the deep truth is imageless" (II, iv, 2–5, 115–16). Insofar as possible he is imageless and voiceless, and it is his function to create the world images decreed by the characters in *Prometheus Unbound* who do possess lyrical voices. Like the inexorable cycle of natural cause and effect embodied in Mont Blanc, which can be construed as either the image of Peacock's tyrant Ahriman or Shelley's intuitions of imaginative love, Demogorgon expresses the generalized quality of lawfulness but not the particulars of any specific law. Order always must be with us, but it is the prerogative of the play's singers to decree what *kind* of order. In the exceptional moment of lyric assertion a character will sing out a new world, and then Demogorgon will make it. He is the linked series of consequences that must follow the primal lyrical impulse—he is the Humean habitual way of seeing that follows the transforming moment of vision. That he embodies law means only that any visionary world must have its own proper order: emphatically, he does not suggest that there is only one world and one law.

Act I: Restraint

The Cenci, which was written between Shelley's composition of the third and fourth acts of *Prometheus Unbound*, is a poetic world which stands as a contrary to the world of Shelley's lyrical drama. If the poet's letter to Peacock merely suggested an alternative world to that of "Mont Blanc," in which the mountain could be interpreted as Ahriman, in *Prometheus Unbound* he actually created the poem that embodies the opposing vision. *Prometheus Unbound* shows moral actions that create world regeneration; *The Cenci* shows moral actions that lead to universal destruction. In my discussion of Act I of *Prometheus Unbound* I will use *The Cenci* as a foil to illuminate the significance of moral action in *Prometheus Unbound*; but although I recognize that *The Cenci* is more complex than I may suggest here, I do not think I have misrepresented it.[3]

Both plays explore the moral problem of tyranny, which is viewed as an unbridled expression of the will. Even though he is Jupiter's victim, in this sense Prometheus is also a tyrant—for the language of his curse expresses a global will to power. He dares Jupiter to "Do thy worst," which includes the right "To blast mankind" with "frost and fire" and "Lightning, and cutting hail" (268–75). Clearly, this world destruction is invoked to prove that Prometheus' will is stronger than Jupiter's; it is a sort of masochistic pride that regards the ability to suffer anything which can be inflicted as superior to the power of inflicting it. Prometheus harbors the arrogance of the heroic victim. In this he resembles Beatrice in *The Cenci*, who has been compelled by her father to commit incest, so that, as he says, "her stubborn will/ . . . by its own consent shall stoop as low/ As that which drags it down" (IV, i, 10–12). But instead of breaking her will, Beatrice's victimization strengthens it, producing an arrogant self-righteousness that will stop at nothing to be avenged. So she turns her own father's tyranny back upon him, countering incest with patricide. Her act is a parody of Cenci's, a failure to transform his moral vision of the world. As she says in despair to her judges, "what a world we make,/ The oppressor and the oppressed" (V, iii, 74–75).

Indeed, *Prometheus Unbound* and *The Cenci* do suggest that the oppressor and the oppressed share a sort of identity, for their actions stem from a shared world vision which exalts the primacy of the will. Both tyrant and victim see human relationships inevitably as power relationships—everything is determined by force or the threat of force; and the object is to achieve domination, which may be won by the victim as well as by the tyrant. In a sense, then, it is irrelevant whether one becomes the tyrant or the victim, for in either case one will respond to the situation as though it were a test of one's will. Further, the global vision of both tyrant and victim involves an implicit notion of *relationship* with another: to be a tyrant, one requires a victim, and to be victimized, one must be overpowered by a tyrant. The minimum number of persons necessary to constitute this world is thus two. The tyrant/victim complex is related to the worlds of all

Shelley's poetry previously discussed in this volume, because in all those poems the number of personages necessary for the creation of a world also is two: the *Alastor* Poet and his dreamed lover, the speaker of "Hymn to Intellectual Beauty" and Beauty, the poet of "Mont Blanc" and the mountain peak, the singer of "Ode to the West Wind" and the West Wind. Of course, in all these cases the two obviously are in another sense one. The point is that poetic imagination is not autonomous—it cannot create absolutely unconditioned worlds. In this regard the imagination is not pure but contingent, not wholly artistic but also moral. To create a world implies the creation of a relationship with another, and to transform a world implies the transformation of one's conduct toward another.[4]

To this point, we have seen that the characteristic Shelleyan transformation is based on a loving relationship. Transforming images mirror the hidden divinity in the self and elicit its articulation into an idealized poetic world. But in *The Cenci*, this sort of transformation is precisely reversed. The play abounds with mirrors, but in no case do they promote idealization. Beatrice herself is a kind of mirror; her brother Bernardo calls her "That perfect mirror of pure innocence/ Wherein I gazed, and grew happy and good." He also calls her the "light of life" (V, iv, 130–32, 134), which as Stuart Curran notices, echoes the acclaim of Asia as "Life of Life" and "Child of Light" in *Prometheus Unbound* (II, v, 48, 54).[5] Like Asia and the other visionary women in Shelley's poetry, Beatrice is a potentially idealizing other. But instead of functioning transformationally, Beatrice mirrors things by merely replicating them. She arms her innocence and refuses to be touched by her father's violation, giving him back exactly what he has given her. Patricide mirrors incest. Beatrice duplicates her father; the "perfect mirror of pure innocence" reflects evil unawares, and herself accomplishes her father's purpose of corruption.

If untouched innocence can be made to reflect evil, then one would think that experience and self-knowledge might be indicated as a moral corrective. But *The Cenci* features experienced, aware characters who are far more reprehensible than Beatrice because they lack her redeeming innocence. Her brother Giacomo looks upon the face of his corruptor Orsino, lamenting that "thy smooth and ready countenance" has been "The mirror of my darkest thoughts," reflecting "the monster of my thought, until/ It grew familiar to desire" (V, i, 20–24). Orsino has functioned as a parody of the transforming image: he is a mirror that allows Giacomo to see his own worst self, a vision that has led to a dark reality. But if neither innocence nor self-knowledge can free the characters of *The Cenci* from evil, then can anything?

It is within this context from *The Cenci* that Prometheus' actions are best understood. Unlike Beatrice, he does not remain innocent of his own impulses, and unlike Giacomo, he does not look within himself to achieve self-knowledge. As Orsino suggests, such "self-anatomy" acquaints us not with our better selves but with "what must be thought, and may be done/ . . . the depth of darkest purposes" (II, ii, 110, 112–13). And so, Act I of *Prometheus Unbound* demonstrates the poetic way of recognizing evil, which is through indirection, through the help of transforming imagery which presents the fact of evil as an external presence which then may be recognized without the danger of self-corruption involved in introspection.[6] Although the point of Prometheus' confrontations of the phantasm of Jupiter and the hallucinatory imagery of the Furies is that he gains novel insights into himself, he never really has to make the demoralizing recognition that "that is me"—instead, he can say, "I do not want to be like that." He confronts himself in the persona of another, a procedure which saves him from the danger of self-contempt.[7]

The phantasm of Jupiter offers the first case in point. Having delivered his curse in blind anger, Prometheus does not remember what he said and needs to listen to his own words again. Jupiter's ghost rather than his own becomes his chosen spokesman, because

Prometheus resists hearing "aught/ Of that which may be evil
pass again/ My lips, or those of aught resembling me" (I, 218–20).
The intention is to use the phantasm disassociatively, to distance
his responsibility for his own song; but as Milton Wilson and
Wasserman have noted, the irony is that the image of Jupiter turns
out to be a perfectly appropriate accompaniment to Prometheus'
lyric curse.[8] What he has sung could have come only from a
persona such as Jupiter, with "gestures proud and cold,/ And
looks of firm defiance, and calm hate" (258–59). Jupiter and
Prometheus are an identity. In recognizing this, however, it is not
necessary to go as far as Wilson and Wasserman and claim that
Jupiter is only an aspect of Prometheus—that the two literally are
an identity. Indeed, Shelley's drama portrays Jupiter as a separate
character who is seized by Demogorgon and dragged down into
the Earth in Act II, scene i. The real point is that Jupiter and
Prometheus share a vision of the world that sees the tyrant/victim
relationship as the only one possible. For although imaginative
experience may be a function of individuals who conceive of the
world in terms of relationship, this does not necessarily imply that
relationship is solely a poetic fiction. On the contrary: poetic
fictions of relationship may help to transform an individual's
actual relationships with others.

Because Prometheus only can conceive of a world populated by
tyrants and victims, he has delivered a prophecy that merely
reverses the present roles: he prays that Jupiter himself will someday become the victim.

> let a sufferer's curse
> Clasp thee, his torturer, like remorse;
> Till thine Infinity shall be
> A robe of envenomed agony;
> And thine Omnipotence a crown of pain,
> To cling like burning gold round thy dissolving brain.
> (286–91)

The imagery suggests Christ's mock elevation as King of the Jews, arrayed in crown of thorns and regal robe, preceding his crucifixion. But nowhere in *Prometheus Unbound* does Jupiter seem to look like this. Rather, the description fits Prometheus himself, whose own phantasm "dost hang, a writhing shade,/ 'Mid whirl-wind-peopled mountains" at the Earth's center (203–4). The posture of the real Prometheus is the same: he hangs "Nailed" to a cliff in the Caucasus, where "The crawling glaciers pierce me with the spears/ Of their moon-freezing crystals" (20, 31).

In fact, as the phantasm of Jupiter repeats Prometheus' curse, the reader of *Prometheus Unbound* sees that two transforming images are in confrontation: the words of Prometheus issue from the mouth of Jupiter, transforming the Titan into the tyrant; and the body of Prometheus hangs nailed to the cliff, transformed into the image of the crucified Christ. This suggests not only the global relationship of tyrant and victim, but the truth that it is Prometheus himself who has decreed this kind of world. The real Jupiter has not been a party to these transformations—they are made possible only by the will of Prometheus himself. He has made his body into a world where both tyranny and suffering are meted out; to attain domination over Jupiter he has defied the god to inflict the extreme of physical punishment. Such willing-ness to mortify his own flesh betrays a terrible self-contempt, a degradation of his physical being to the ends decreed by his implacable will. This contempt relates to his perceived world as well as to his body: the Firebringer has goaded Jupiter "To blast mankind" as well as himself, bringing destruction to the human race merely to prove the heroism of his defiance.

Although the reader of *Prometheus Unbound* can trace all these relationships, it is not necessary for Prometheus himself to do so. He need not be aware of his role in creating the transforming images, and indeed, it is better that he is not. What he does come to understand is how tyranny looks and sounds. Voice and image seem to stand apart from him as an other, and in this form they may be observed. That is, the confrontation between Prometheus and these images is analogous to the Shelleyan poet's confrontation with his own poem. Although it is true that the Shelleyan poem is a transformed image of the poet, this does not mean that the poem should collapse back into the poet's self. On the contrary—only when the poem stands apart, when indirection is preserved, can the poet see himself in the particular way poetry makes possible.

So Prometheus' entirely adequate response is merely, "It doth repent me . . ./ I wish no living thing to suffer pain" (303–5). He abjures the very idea of force, which is the basis of the tyrant/ victim world view. However, the reign of Jupiter continues in the long stretches of Act I still remaining. Why does this happen? It is because, as the visitation of the Furies makes clear, the wish that *no one* experience pain under *any* circumstances is an imprecise and overemphatic formulation of Prometheus' new willing. The Furies come to administer a "cup of pain" (474), and like Christ, Prometheus has the option to refuse it. But if he does so, he will have refused the kind of pain that Christ accepted to save the world. Such suffering is the very opposite of self-contempt. Instead of being a torture imposed on a part of the self by one's own unbending will, this new pain is the pain of a novel kind of self-recognition, the realization of the evil and weakness that one shares in community with all mankind. This experience is precisely the one avoided by Beatrice in *The Cenci*. As Prometheus says to the Furies after they have done their worst, "Thy words are like a cloud of wingèd snakes;/ And yet I pity those they torture not" (632–33). Beatrice would be the perfect candidate for such pity: an innocent blinded by self-righteousness, who commits an evil act because she cannot recognize herself as capable of evil. If she had had a sense of her own susceptibility to evil very possibly Beatrice could have set a watch over herself. Instead, she often displays a sense of superiority over the good but weak characters in the play, such as her stepmother and younger brother; and when her hired assassins confess their guilt under torture she is unforgiving—for she would not have so acted herself. In Beatrice we see the tendency of the good person to take dangerous pride in his individual will; she denies relationship with erring humanity.

Prometheus' incarnation as the crucified Christ is an acceptance that is the contrary of Beatrice's inflexibility. The crucified Christ is the god who took on human form, who forsook the prerogatives of godhead in order to become part of the human enterprise and transform it. Like Christ, Prometheus will not lift himself above the human race. The Furies try to make him do so, by showing him a hopeful revolution, much like the French Revolution, which eventually betrays its promise and ends in a bloodbath; and next, a religious poet, much like Christ, who creates a bright new moral vision which after his death is betrayed viciously by the church founded in his name. Both scenes are demonstrations of the Furies' hypothesis—that man's efforts to better his world always will lead to destruction. If this is true, hope certainly should be abandoned, for it is a harmful delusion. But if Prometheus assents to this proposition he will be abandoning hope for himself as well as for humanity, because his failing has been precisely analogous to theirs: the Firebringer gave gifts to the human race and then turned and blasted the world with his curse. He has been no better than struggling mankind for whom the Furies show such contempt.

This is made evident by the transformational nature of the Furies' imagery. They picture not the inevitable way of the world, but the way Prometheus himself fears the world goes. Their visions come from Prometheus' heart; like the vultures that daily tear at Prometheus' liver in Aeschylus' *Prometheus Bound*, these Shelleyan Furies feed upon whatever is already present in their victim. As one says, "from our victim's destined agony/ The shade which is our form invests us round;/ Else are we shapeless as our mother Night" (470–72). Additionally, the Furies work in silence—they are not lyrical beings. As one says to his fellow, "Speak not: whisper not: . . . to speak might break the spell" (533–35). Presumably, they then go on to create a panorama of silent pictures. Although it is true that Prometheus and Panthea and Ione hear groans during the torture, these groans could be either the groans of mankind or Prometheus—and in fact, they are the groans of both. It is Prometheus who must decree the world order, and so the Furies' silent imagery is a kind of trick designed to convince him that he must despair because he is powerless, when in fact it is only he who has the primal lyrical power.

The lyrical restraint exercised by Prometheus in this scene becomes crucial. He must avoid assenting to his own fears and weakness, for if he gives in he will have decreed a new lyrical world order which will be an even more fallen world than the present one. But necessary as it is, such restraint only can prevent degeneration, it cannot create improvement. For that, Prometheus is required to exhibit a heroic virtue that is the complementary opposite to his restraint—uninhibited compassion for the suffering he sees. He does so most dramatically in his confrontation of the Furies' image of Christ. Agonized by the dying god's pain, he impulsively reaches out to him, crying, "let that thorn-wounded brow/ Stream not with blood . . . O horrible!" (598–603).

In feeling Christ's pain so vividly he is feeling his own—for he too is the incarnation of Christ. Earlier, the crucified Prometheus confronted the phantasm of Jupiter, a pairing that suggested the intimate global relationship of tyrant and victim. Now the pairing of the crucified Prometheus and the crucified Christ suggests the global relationship of pain and compassion. Without realizing it, in feeling a ready sympathy for Christ's suffering Prometheus also is feeling sympathy for himself. The imperious being who crucified himself by the language of his own curse, compelling himself to wear the "robe of envenomed agony" and "crown of

pain," now feels the horror of pain and impulsively reaches out to
the sufferer. This gesture dramatically suggests that self-love can
be a transformational emotion born out of our concern for others. Just as in *The Cenci* Orsino counsels the avoidance of "self-
anatomy" because it brings to light "what must be thought, and
may be done/ . . . the depths of darkest purposes," (II, ii, 112–13)
so also we can see that an introspective self-love easily could lead
to monstrous egotism, a valuing of self above the rest of the
world. In fact, that is Beatrice's sin: she loves her own goodness
altogether too well and thereby isolates herself from the human
community. For Shelley, self-love can be valid only through the
poetry of transformation, which finds its beloved through a conversion of the self into the world. Instead of walling ourselves off
from others, we must reach out selflessly to embrace them. As
he says in the *Defence*: "The great secret of morals is love; or a
going out of our own nature, and an identification of ourselves
with the beautiful which exists in thought, action, or person, not
our own. A man, to be greatly good, must imagine intensely and
comprehensively; he must put himself in the place of another
and of many others . . ." (VII, 118). In embracing Christ, Prometheus embraces himself and transforms himself into Christ.
Therefore, he saves his world.

That salvation indeed is in the air is suggested by the Chorus of
Spirits which materializes after the Furies' disappearance. They
come from "the dim caves of human thought" and "inhabit, as
birds wing the wind/ Its world-surrounding aether" (659–60).
Such places exist only in thought, not in nature; they are transformations of natural forms. These Spirits herald the heaven of
Shelleyan culture. They have witnessed destruction as terrible as
that depicted by the Furies—shipwreck, tyranny, war—but they
have seen these disasters transformed by the self-sacrifice of men
who cherish hopes for a more humane future. Such hope is a faith
in the transformational power of man to create the good he
imagines.

The Spirits' celebration of the poet, that prime Shelleyan cultural hero, emphasizes the power of transformation with particular clarity. He spends his days contemplating the beauties of nature but will not "heed nor see, what things they be;/ But from these create he can/ Forms more real than living man,/ Nurslings of immortality!" (746–49). As in the *Defence*, here the poet is "unacknowledged legislator of the world." Although he seems not to labor, actually he performs the most important human work of all: the creation of poetry, the imagination of an ideal human order which can provide the inspiration for change in actual human life. The merely natural, impulsive hatred that wrecked Prometheus' world at one blow can be countered only by the incessant imaginations of poetry, which forever renew the structure of human culture.

Act II: Surrender

In the poetic world of *Prometheus Unbound*, the opposite and complementary action to restraint is surrender. Where restraint begins with an increased capacity to see, to interpret images that mirror the self, surrender begins with an increased capacity to feel, to be carried away by images that well up from inside. Dreams teach one to desire, which is to reach out beyond one's inner self into the world, in hopes of embracing the incarnation of one's imaginings.

Just as the tyrannical world view of Act I implied a global relationship between tyrants and victims, so the dreams that initiate Act II imply a global relationship between lovers. In both cases, the individual imagination creates a world by making itself two—by positing a fundamental mode of relationship. Thus, when Asia pursues her dreams, she is acting within a poetic fiction of twoness, within a world of imagery, that indirectly embodies herself. Although the aura of necessitarianism in this Act is powerful, the necessity involved is neither the materialistic

necessitarianism suggested by *Queen Mab* nor the Humean necessitarianism of habit. Rather, in following out her own dreams
Asia follows herself—her journey is the exfoliation of her own
extraordinary imaginings, the actualization in space and time of
her own dream imagery. As in "Mont Blanc," where the cryptic
transforming image must be interpreted through the poet's articulation, Asia's dreams must be made real by her own activity. The
speaker of "Mont Blanc" creates a poem, and in Shelley's play
Asia creates the fictional analogue of a poem—she makes a new
world.

The opening scene of the Act, in which Asia and Panthea
discuss their dreams, hypothesizes a world of love through the
central image of Prometheus as the transfigured Christ. If the
crucified Christ symbolized the victim who was a necessary part
of the tyrannical world view, in Panthea's dream of Prometheus
we have that same Christ arisen. He is the very type of transformation: in the Bible his "face did shine as the sun, and his raiment
was white as the light" (Matthew 17:2), and in Panthea's dream
"his pale wound-worn limbs/ Fell from Prometheus, and the
azure night/ Grew radiant with the glory of that form/ Which lives
unchanged within" (II, i, 62–65). As he spoke to Panthea, the
love radiating from his eyes and lips "Steamed forth like vaporous
fire, an atmosphere/ Which wrapped me in its all-dissolving
power,/ As the warm ether of the morning sun/ Wraps ere it
drinks some cloud of wandering dew" (75–78). Although the
obvious quality of this dream is erotic, it expresses a great deal
more than that. Panthea feels desire; she is drawn outside herself
into a communion with someone else, so intense that it becomes a
new form of extreme inwardness. As she says to Asia of her
dream, "I am made the wind/ Which fails beneath the music that I
bear/ Of thy most wordless converse; since dissolved/ Into the
sense with which love talks" (50–53). Panthea feels she is the
representative of Asia and that the "wordless converse" of the
dream is the communion between Asia and Prometheus.

But the inwardness and silence of dreams is not self-sufficient; Ione, who vaguely has sensed Panthea's dream in her own sleep, awakes and exclaims in perplexity:

> Canst thou divine what troubles me tonight?
> I always knew what I desired before,
> Nor ever found delight to wish in vain.
> But now I cannot tell thee what I seek;
> I know not . . .
>   . . . when just now
> We kissed, I felt within thy parted lips
> The sweet air that sustained me; and the warmth
> Of the life-blood, for loss of which I faint,
> Quivered between our intertwining arms.
>
>   (94–106)

Panthea's dream, which was permeated with the atmosphere of Prometheus' radiant eyelight and breath, makes Ione feel as though her own breath has been stolen away. This is because the dream creates a vision of fulfillment rather than a reality, and so the awakened sleeper experiences restlessness—a newly created desire, but for what, she does not know clearly. Where in 1815 Shelley portrayed such a dream as blighting the *Alastor* Poet's life, turning him away from engagement with the world and leading him to death, in *Prometheus Unbound* such dreams produce an opposite effect. What simply happens in Panthea's dream must be *made* to happen in the waking world. Her dream becomes a transformational phenomenon, for it draws her into action, into a search for the meaning with which the vision has been mysteriously saturated—saturated, but not formulated.

However, in another sense the evocative quality of dreams is due to their excessive, rather than inadequate, degree of formulation. Panthea's dream is "read" (110) by Asia, who looking into her eyes, sees Panthea's dream of the sunlike Prometheus transformed into an image of "the cloud-surrounded moon" who briefly "smiles" at her and then disappears (121–22). This is followed by the appearance of a form with "rude hair" which "Roughens the wind that lifts it, its regard/ Is wild and quick, yet 'tis a thing of air" (127–29). In turn, the airy imperativeness of this figure reminds Panthea of another of her dreams, in which a wind blew away blossoms from an almond tree, and on each petal "was stamped . . . O FOLLOW, FOLLOW" (139, 141). That dream then reminds Asia of her own, which also was of a breezy world in which clouds and leaves impressed with those words "FOLLOW, O, FOLLOW" were swept along by the spring winds (153, 159, 162). This fabric of multiple dream images is reminiscent of Shelley's poetic technique in "Hymn to Intellectual Beauty." There the artist tries to cope with his feeling through the use of not one image but many; for the proliferation of images, like the proliferation of the Nereids' dream, provides a wealth of material that tentatively formulates the difficult intuitions which are the subject of the poem. Similarly, although Asia is presented with many dreams, she can sense an intuitional cohesion in them which she cannot yet explain.

But as Panthea and Asia continue to discuss these dreams, the efforts at analysis give way to their rising tide of enthusiasm. No matter what these images mean, they certainly do elicit excitement and desire. So as the Nereids continue to speak of them, their voices presumably intensify and grow louder—until suddenly, the dream-command, "FOLLOW, FOLLOW!," returns to them as a lyrical echo (163). It is the voice of their own desire, projected into the world and made into an other. At this important point, image has been transformed into song. The inwardness and silence of dreams has elicited a voice of lyric longing which fills the world and echoes back to the singer, making what originates in the self appear to have come from outside. Although she may not realize it, Asia now follows her own echoed song. Her expression of desire, born of her own dreams, becomes the lyric foil to Prometheus' curse: it begins to create the world anew, in the form of love.

But if the song of desire initiates world transformation in Act II of *Prometheus Unbound*, it is nevertheless obvious that a natural transformation also is underway. Spring is coming, and its first freshening winds are blowing everywhere. Is the juxtaposition of spring and Asia's song simply an effort at poetic decor on Shelley's part, or does the world structure of *Prometheus Unbound* yield a poetic law that binds these phenomena together? Here, a fragment probably connected with the *Defence* offers a useful perspective:

> In one mode of considering these two classes of action of the human mind which are called reason and imagination, the former may be considered as mind employed upon the relations borne by one thought to another, however produced, and imagination as mind combining the elements of thought itself. It has been termed the power of association; and on an accurate anatomy of the functions of the mind, it would be difficult to assign any other origin to the mass of what we perceive and know than this power. Association is, however, rather a law according to which this power is exerted than the power itself; in the same manner as gravitation is a passive expression of the reciprocal tendency of heavy bodies towards their respective centres. Were these bodies conscious of such a tendency, the name which they would assign to that consciousness would express the cause of gravitation; and it were a vain inquiry as to what might be the cause of that cause. Association bears the same relation to imagination as a mode to a source of action. . . .
>
> (VII, 107)

Shelley relates the psychological law of association to the physical law of gravitation because both are ways of formulating phenomena by the method of reason. From the reasonable perspective, one derives "passive expression[s]" of "mode[s]"—that is, exterior descriptions of the ways components in any system fit together, rather than an interior "consciousness" of the synthetic energies involved. But were physical bodies "conscious . . . the name they would assign to that consciousness would express the cause of gravitation"—which indeed does happen in Act IV of *Prometheus Unbound*, with the lyrical dance of the Earth and the Moon. There, the planets call that cause love. Something similar happens in Act II. What we witness is a living world coming to a newborn consciousness of its name, which also is love. In *Prometheus Unbound* Shelley has transformed the laws of nature poetically, so that they become the expression not of reason but of imagination. As in "Ode to the West Wind," the winds of nature have entered the poet's mind and emerged transformed into poetry. Wind and song, then, become dual aspects of a transformational unity.

Indeed, this fundamental poetic law of *Prometheus Unbound* accounts for the entire imagistic order of the play: everywhere, Shelley has used the notion of natural necessity to body forth the imperatives of his poetic necessity. For example, Asia's and Panthea's dreams are filled with images derived from the natural interaction of wind, water, and sunlight. In Panthea's dream of Prometheus, he is a sun which draws her upward as though she were "some cloud of wandering dew" (78), but her vaporous being condenses when he disappears, and she falls to earth, "Gathering again in drops upon the pines" (84). Here the processes of evaporation and condensation emerge into a kind of kinesthetic self-consciousness which can be called desire. Similarly, the dreams of following are physical: the cry, "O FOLLOW, FOLLOW," that in Asia's dream appears on the clouds and blossoms and in Panthea's liquid eyes is the song voiced by moisture drawn toward vaporization by the wind. The enactment of Asia's dreams also is expressed by the physical process of evaporation. Airy Spirits see Asia and Panthea passing like "some cloud of dew,/ Drifted along the earth-creeping breeze" (II, ii, 7–8) or like "inland boats . . . driven to Ocean/ Down streams made strong with mountain-thaw" (45–46). They say that beings thus driven "float upon their way,/ Until, still sweet, but loud and strong,/ The storm of song is driven along,/ Sucked up and hurrying" (57–60), suggesting that moving wind and water gradually come to self-consciousness as a lyrical storm of sound. When Asia and Panthea pause at the brink of Demogorgon's volcanic flue, they are surrounded by a "wide plain of billowy mist" (II, iii, 19); in the midst of it appear spirits which beckon them downward "As the lightning the vapour" (66), making them condense as Panthea did when Prometheus disappeared in her dream; but this journey downward is much more fearful, for it takes Asia into Demogorgon's mountain, where the vapors are not evaporated dew but poisonous volcanic gases. When she again rises into the world from her subterranean ordeal, Asia herself is transformed; seeing her, Panthea asks, "whence is the light/ Which fills the cloud? the sun is yet unrisen" (II, v, 8–9). Panthea's dream of Prometheus as the sun has been fulfilled by the radiant, cloudlike Asia, who through her desire for him has transformed herself into the image of her own love. In terms of the Act's physical imagery, she has become the wind and sunlight as well as the water; in the great transformational process of spring she has played the parts of both subject and agent.

As G. M. Matthews and Wasserman have suggested, the imagery of Act I also expresses a transformation of the natural world into a world of imagination. In this perspective, exhaustively discussed in Wasserman's chapter "The Breathing Earth," Prometheus' curse becomes the voice of a volcano, and his breath becomes poisonous fumes that cover his world after the volcanic eruption.[9] The Furies become volcanic clouds that issue from the diseased Earth to "burthen the blast of the atmosphere" (I, 519), and the imagery they produce for Prometheus is the hallucinations caused by breathing poisoned volcanic gases. In Act II this noxious world atmosphere gradually is retracted into the Earth's center, and the fresh winds of spring are breathed out to replace it. Then in Act IV, as we shall see, the liberated creativity of human nature works upon purified natural forms to transform them into the Shelleyan paradise of civilization.

As in "Ode to the West Wind," this poetic transformation of the laws of nature provides both a sense of being swept up into belief in the inevitable revolution and a simultaneous recognition that such belief lives within the boundaries of a poetic world. The play's necessitarianism becomes a poetic transformation of materialistic necessitarianism, for it enacts not a literal system of the world, but the imagination's necessary creation of what it itself desires. The imagination's strivings must be incarnated in order to be affirmed, and the aesthetic power of Shelley's play lies in its ability to express this imaginative law through the solid and convincing inevitability of physical process.

Thus, spirit becomes wind, water, and sunlight, and in that form is made visible to us. It assumes a body, it can become a world—the world of *Prometheus Unbound*. Shelley's drama is a poetic world that gains force by its material imaginings but never can be brought to the stage. Its embodiment cannot be through the bodies of actors, but only by the imaginative transformation of the poet's spirit into the world. As with Shelley's other poems, *Prometheus Unbound* converts the universe into a poetic universe —it is an imaginary world that indirectly mirrors the poet's self. Although Shelley has written a drama, as the subtitle suggests, it is a "Lyrical Drama." In his hands, the drama has been transformed into the lyric. Itself transformational, this work also has transformed genres.

A word remains to be said about Asia's meeting with Demogorgon. As Wasserman points out, this scene probably is modeled on Aeneas' visit to the underworld in Book VI of the Æneid.[10] There Aeneas goes to visit his dead father, Anchises, who supplies him with a panoramic view of the future, including Aeneas' founding of Rome and the entire history of the Roman state. But before he enters the underworld he asks for the guidance of the

Cumaean Sibyl, who inhabits an oracular cave and prophesies when possessed by Apollo. On this occasion "Her hair stood up; convulsive rage possessed/ Her trembling limbs, and heaved her laboring breast."[11] This brutal possession perhaps is recalled in Panthea's musings as she regards Demogorgon's cave, which is "Like a volcano's meteor-breathing chasm,/ Whence the oracular vapor is hurled up." Men breathing this poisonous vapor become possessed by visions and madly sing out "Like Maenads who cry loud, Evoe! Evoe!/ The voice which is contagion to the world" (II, iii, 3–10). The lyricism of such men is as blind as the lyricism of Prometheus' curse and can produce a similar kind of poetic catastrophe. The safeguard against such destruction is the understanding that one's visions are not oracular communications from some external god but the indirect manifestation of one's own imaginative life. And so, Asia comes to realize that Demogorgon cannot deliver an authoritative interpretation of her visions. He remains imageless and nearly voiceless, giving only cryptic replies to her persistent questionings—for unlike Vergil's Anchises, he has no prophetic knowledge. At last Asia sees that she herself must interpret her own world and does so, saying that all things can be subject to love, and "of such truths/ Each to itself must be the oracle" (II, iv, 122–23). Immediately she is charioted into the upper world and transfigured. Thus, the processes of Shelley's underworld are exactly the opposite of Vergil's, for instead of prophesying the future, Demogorgon simply enacts the promise of the past, which was born in Panthea's dream of Prometheus.

The implications are clear: the imagination is a law unto itself and its dreamings are its own cryptic predictions, which it must interpret in order to fulfill. In Asia's case, however, the dream prediction involves a significant inaccuracy. Panthea dreamed of a transfigured Prometheus, but the fulfillment of the prophecy turns out to be Asia's own transfiguration. After all, this is the imaginative truth: our dreams may be of a world made anew, but if we live them out truly, we become like "fountain-gazing roses" (II, v, 13), ourselves transfigured in the transforming mirror of our own creations. As in Shelley's other poetry, the transformation of a world has ended in the indirect transformation of that world's maker.

Act IV: Creation

Act IV was added a few months after Shelley finished the rest of the play. I believe that it presents an alternative to the first ending of the drama seen in Act III, which was needed because the third act does not satisfactorily portray the transformed world Prometheus and Asia have created by their labors.

What would the poetic texture of such a world be? In Act III Shelley answers this question by extending the narrative developed in his first two acts: Prometheus would be unbound and reunited with Asia, and the volcanic disruption of the earth would cease, leaving a world in which all things would emerge in their own loveliness. But this merely narrative ending ignores the transformational structure of Shelley's "Lyrical Drama." A glance at Act III shows the conspicuous surface of the problem: this is the only act that contains no lyrics at all. In contrast, a count of lyrical lines versus narrative lines in the rest of the play reveals that Act I is rather less than one part lyrical to one part narrative,[12] Act II is about one part lyrical to two parts narrative,[13] and Act IV is quite predominantly lyrical—about three parts lyrical to one part narrative.[14] From this perspective, the unlyrical Act III emerges as an anomaly.

When one looks at how lyricism and narration function in the first two acts, one discovers that the drama's most intense articulations are all lyrical—expressions such as Prometheus' curse, the Furies' temptation, the comfort given by the Spirits in Act I, and in Act II, the songs that draw Asia and Panthea forward, and the supreme lyrics "Life of Life" and "My soul is an enchanted boat" that celebrate Asia's transfiguration. These lyrical parts of the play belong to beings who are involved entirely in their own ongoing actions. In contrast, Act III divorces expression from action. Prior to the act's opening, the Spirit of the Hour has circled the earth, trumpeting in the new order, and the act itself simply shows him reporting what he already has done.

Instead of witnessing world transformation, in Act III we are presented with a *fait accompli*. A world of already achieved perfection, the milieu of the act offers no further possibilities for significant doing. It is a static paradise, a fact uncomfortably revealed by the artistic transformation of Prometheus, Asia, Panthea, Ione, and the Earth into commemorative statuary enshrined in a heavenly temple, eternally to mark the Spirit of the Hour's completed transfiguration of the world. Within this temple his horses "will live exempt from toil,/ Pasturing flowers of vegetable fire" (III, iv, 109–10). The living Prometheus and Asia also are put out to pasture in this act; they "will entangle buds and flowers and beams/ Which twinkle on the fountain's brim, and make/ Strange combinations out of common things,/ Like human babes in their brief innocence" (III, iii, 30–33). Creation has degenerated into pretty hobbyism, and the creators have ascended into the cold marble of a heavenly museum.[15]

It is a peculiar apotheosis for the poet who in his *Defence of Poetry* compared the mind in creation to a fading coal, and added that "when composition begins, inspiration is already on the decline, and the most glorious poetry that has ever been communicated to the world is probably a feeble shadow of the original conceptions of the Poet" (VII, 135). When he is true to himself, Shelley values the act of creation more highly than the produced work. It follows that his proper heaven should be a place where consciousness is eternally creating itself. A Shelleyan heaven would involve energy sufficient to support continual intuition and lyric power sufficient to express it continually. Like Shelley's skylark, the ultimate poet would exist entirely in the present, where his song would become one with his evolving self-consciousness.

> Hail to thee, blithe Spirit!
>   Bird thou never wert—
> That from Heaven, or near it,
>   Pourest thy full heart
> In profuse strains of unpremeditated art.

Like the skylark, the singers in Act IV of *Prometheus Unbound* raise "strains of unpremeditated art"; and yet the result is not a formless outpouring but the creation of a new world. "We whirl, singing loud, round the gathering sphere,/ Till the trees, and the beasts, and the clouds appear" (169–71). At the heart of Act IV is the confidence that spontaneity and order can be combined in the lyrical unfolding of consciousness. For like Wordsworth, Shelley believes in the ideal of "spontaneous overflow of powerful feelings." But as soon as Wordsworth coins this phrase in the Preface to the *Lyrical Ballads*, he adds: "Poems to which any value can be attached, were never produced on any variety of subjects but by a man who being possessed of more than usual organic sensibility had also thought long and deeply. For our continued influxes of feeling are modified and directed by our thoughts, which are indeed the representatives of all our past feelings."[16] Because the lyric present is the flowering of the singer's entire past, it becomes important for Wordsworth to understand the history of the poet's mind. Hence, *The Prelude*. In this Wordsworthian perspective *Prometheus Unbound* also emerges as an account of the growth of the poetic mind, from the expulsion of its own devils in Act I, to the surrender to its own desires in Act II, to its finally achieved power of lyric creation in Act IV. The lyric exuberance of Act IV depends upon the achievements of Acts I and II and could not exist without them. The song that seems effortless and "unpremeditated" is actually the fruit of heroic suffering and self-surrender.

So the ideal lyric present is not a separate moment of rapture but a transformation of the singer's past life into a unified order which is continually evolving. Since it is both spontaneous and orderly, such a song masters time. Where in Act I Prometheus was the suffering slave of time, enduring "moments aye divided by keen pangs/ Till they seemed years" (13–14), the Hours and Spirits in Act IV can make time do their bidding. Through their "mystic measure/ Of music, and dance" (77–78) they can render time "Ceaseless, and rapid, and fierce, and free" or "Solemn, and slow, and serene, and bright" (163–66). The rhythms of dance and poetry can become the rhythms of time itself, for as Shelley said of the phenomenal flow of experience in a note to *Queen Mab*,

> Time is our consciousness of the succession of ideas in our mind. Vivid sensation, of either pain or pleasure, makes the time seem long, as the common phrase is, because it renders us more acutely conscious of our ideas. If a mind be conscious of a hundred ideas during one minute by the clock, and of two hundred during another, the latter of these spaces would actually occupy so much greater extent in the mind as two exceed one in quantity. If therefore, the human mind, by any future improvement of its sensibility, should become conscious of an infinite number of ideas in a minute, that minute would be eternity. I do not hence infer that the actual space between the birth and death of a man will ever be prolonged; but that his sensibility is perfectible, and that the number of ideas which his mind is capable of receiving is indefinite.
>
> (I, 156–57)

In this view, infinity is available within clock time if every moment of that time is lived fully. This clarifies the nature of the lyric moment: not only is it a transformation of the past, it also is the present lived as completely as possible. It is pure action, and that is why it is dramatic. As Shelley says in a poem appended to this *Queen Mab* note, "The sense of love,/ The thirst for action, and the impassioned thought/ Prolong my being." [17]

If the ideal lyric masters time, it also controls space. In Act II spirit was incarnated in space, as Asia and Panthea became wind, water, sunlight, air, and cloud—they transformed the world's body by infusing it with joyful self-consciousness. This physical transformation intensifies in Act IV. The singing Spirits and Hours become like "some soft cloud" which "vanishes into rain" (182), and their chorus sings, "Let the Hours, and the spirits of might and pleasure,/ Like the clouds and sunbeams, unite" (79–80). The winds, waters, and sunlight that in Act II combined to create the necessitarian sequence of spring here are liberated to control their own structures and their own time. Their song and dance rhythmically transform nature into a world-poem. Appropriately, they "will take our plan/ From the new world of man,/ And our work shall be called the Promethean" (156–58). Although Prometheus does not appear in this act, it is true to his spirit: the Firebringer improved upon nature and so do these singers.

The space created by the lyricists continually expands outward from their expressive centers. As clouds, vapors, and sunlight in a "storm of delight . . . panic of glee!" (44) they physically enlarge by vaporization. Similarly, the Earth feels a "boundless, over-flowing, bursting gladness,/ The vaporous exultation not to be confined!" (320–21). This physical action is emanative: vaporous song radiates from the centers of all living creatures to create an ever-expanding atmosphere, an ambience, that fills the world. Hence, the lyric impulse, which has mastered time and rendered it infinite, also masters space and renders it infinite. For where time can express the fullness of imaginative action, space can express the immensity of imaginative scope. The *Defence* employs a similar image of expansion from an expressive center: "Poetry enlarges the circumference of the imagination by replenishing it with thoughts of ever new delight, which have the power of attracting and assimilating to their own nature all other thoughts, and which form new intervals and interstices whose void forever craves fresh food . . ." (VII, 117–18). Ideal imaginative time must be infinite because the song which creates it must continue evolving forever, and ideal imaginative space must be infinite because the images which fill it must continue proliferating forever.

But world transformation is not physically expressed only by the dance of the Hours and Spirits. Their lyric vaporization is compelling but airy; what remains to be seen is the transformation of solider forms. Hence, the cosmic dance of the Earth and Moon which follows. If the dance of the Spirits expresses the imagination's lightness, this dance expresses the imagination's weight, power, and incisiveness. As Shelley suggested in his rejected opening of the *Defence*, if the forces of gravitation could come to self-consciousness and name themselves, that name would express the cause of gravity.[18] In Act IV this name is love. Here, gravitation becomes the spatial expression of desire, which penetrates to the very core of the beloved and changes him utterly. Such penetration is at the same time sexual and spiritual, for imagination transforms the world's body by bestowing ecstatic self-awareness upon it. The Moon cries, "Some Spirit is darted like a beam from thee,/ Which penetrates my frozen frame,/ And passes with the warmth of flame,/ With love, and odour, and deep melody/ Through me, through me!" (327–31). In turn, the Earth feels the Moon's force; "It interpenetrates my granite mass,/ Through tangled roots and trodden clay doth pass/ Into the utmost leaves and delicatest flowers" (370–72). The imaginative complement of the Spirits' airy expansiveness is the Earth's and Moon's deep innerness: while the Spirits transform space, the planets transform the heart.

As the song of the Spirits and the Hours combined spontaneity

and order, so does this dance of the planets. Rapturous transformational energies radiate from within the Earth and the Moon,
but they are balanced in a perfect gravitational pairing that at the
same time permits unrestricted expressiveness and absolute control. Thus, the dance of love that completes *Prometheus Unbound*
becomes the dramatic foil for the curse which initiated it. Unrestrained hatred had destroyed the world, but unrestrained love
redeems it—because whereas hatred precipitates chaos, love creates its own self-regulating order. Love is seen to be the heart of
civilization, which the Earth extols as "one harmonious soul of
many a soul,/ Whose nature is its own divine control" (400–1).
Similarly, the ideal human being becomes a self-balanced cosmos:

> His will—with all mean passions, bad delights,
> And selfish cares, its trembling satellites,
> A spirit ill to guide, but mighty to obey—
> Is as a tempest-winged ship, whose helm
> Love rules, through waves which dare not overwhelm,
> Forcing life's wildest shores to own its sovereign sway.
>
> (406–11)

I suspect Shelley has the *Essay on Man* in mind here, and especially
Pope's declaration that "On life's vast ocean diversely we sail,/
Reason the card, but Passion is the gale." The faculty psychology
suggested by Pope's lines implies the necessity of properly sub-
ordinating separate human powers within the hierarchy of the
personality. When Pope extends such a view to embrace human
society and the natural order, the result is the cosmic hierarchy
which he calls the Great Chain of Being. In Act II of *Prometheus
Unbound* the despairing Asia asks Demogorgon about this kind of
chain: "And who made terror, madness, crime, remorse,/ Which
from the links of the great chain of things/ To every thought
within the mind of man/ Sway and drag heavily" (iv, 19–22).
Clearly, the hierarchical model of personality and society im-
presses Shelley as tyrannical. Man is not an assemblage of separate

functions to be governed by subordination, but a world made coherent by the gravitation of his love; and his culture is a divine cosmos, a transformation of nature.

Indeed, it is the voice of civilization that we hear singing in this act—for just as Mont Blanc cannot actually speak, and the West Wind cannot actually hear, the Earth and Moon of *Prometheus Unbound* cannot sing. The world-song we overhear is a transformation of nature, the human possession of the world through its conversion into a poetic universe. Hence, this heaven actually is the heaven of human culture. This ideal transformation obviously has revolutionary social as well as artistic implications.

For both revolution and artistic creation are transformations that begin with the imagination, as Demogorgon emphasizes at the act's end. He issues not from the subterranean cave of Act II, but as "a mighty Power, which is as darkness,/ . . . rising out of Earth, and from the sky/ . . . showered like night, and from within the air/ Bursts, like eclipse which had been gathered up/ Into the pores of sunlight" (510–14). Like the Hours and the Spirits, he is a penetrating vapor simultaneously welling up from every point in the lyrical cosmos, and hence, the master of that world's space and time. He temporarily eclipses the new Creation in order to remind it that only "Gentleness, Virtue, Wisdom, and Endurance" can "bar the pit over Destruction's strength," containing the serpent within that continually threatens world chaos (562–64). This barred pit with its serpent comes from Revelation 20: 1–3, where the promised millennium is to be followed by a time when the snake Satan "must be loosed a little season" to prepare for the apocalypse.[19]

Unlike the prophet of Revelation, Shelley does not see apocalyptic destruction of the world as either necessary or inevitable. His ideal consummation is not the absolute ending of the world but its indefinite continuation. He believes in the millennium because the millennium involves ever-continuing process, ever-continuing evolution, openness.[20] In his ideal lyrical cosmos, song

continually must create time and space; the implication is that
the singers forever must be responsible for what they sing and
become. At any point in the phenomenal flow of time and space
the universe that comes into being in Act IV can be negated,
transformed into a quite different world by singing a different
kind of song—which the ubiquitous Demogorgon immediately
would actualize. In one sense, *Prometheus Unbound* has come very
far beyond Prometheus' curse by creating an entirely new world
that repeals it; but in another, it might be very close to a renewal
of the fall. For that, the singing of an angry song would suffice, a
truth which the pervasive presence of Demogorgon underlines.
He is always present behind the flow of phenomena, capable at
any point of transforming the world's form. Demogorgon's om-
nipresent appearance at the end of *Prometheus Unbound* serves a
function similar to the skeptical questions that end "Mont Blanc"
and "Ode to the West Wind": the poet has swept us up into his
song of hope, but his final words remind us that it is our responsibility to affirm and maintain it. Inevitable as it may sound, his
poem is not a necessary world—it is a vision of ideal possibility.

NOTES

1. See Susan Hawk Brisman, "'Unsaying His High Language': The
Problem of Voice in *Prometheus Unbound*," *SIR* 16, no. 1 (Winter 1977),
pp. 51–86. Brisman argues for a conception of language in *Prometheus
Unbound* in which existence is a function of expression, as I do also in this
chapter. But what she has in mind is the "legacy of Miltonic Satanism,"
which involves "the notion that 'high language' must be founded on
heroic defiance of authority. The question posed by *Prometheus Unbound*,
where the Titan early recants his curse on Jupiter, is whether Shelley can
sustain a language of the sublime once the recantation has precipitated
those impurities of pride, hatred, and contempt that stimulated, even as
they stained, Prometheus' courage never to submit or yield" (p. 81). In
contrast, I will argue that an analysis of lyrical, rather than sublime,
language is closer to the central concerns of *Prometheus Unbound*.
2. Frederick L. Jones attempts a comprehensive listing of Shelley's

references to Milton in "Shelley and Milton," *SP* 49, no. 3 (July 1952), pp. 488–519. He assembles an extensive catalogue of verbal echoes from *Paradise Lost* in *Prometheus Unbound*, but does not mention *Samson Agonistes*.

3. For other comparisons of *Prometheus Unbound* and *The Cenci*, see Stuart Curran, "The Rule of Ahriman," in *Shelley's Annus Mirabilis: The Maturing of an Epic Vision* (San Marino, Calif., 1975), pp. 119–54, and Milton Wilson, "The Temptations of Prometheus," in *Shelley's Later Poetry: A Study of His Prophetic Imagination* (New York, 1959), pp. 71–101.

4. In *The Ringers in the Tower: Studies in Romantic Tradition* (Chicago and London, 1971), Harold Bloom sees connections between Shelley's myth of relationship and Blake's. "A unitary Man fell, and split into torturing and tortured components, and into separated male and female forms as well. The Torturer is not in himself a representative of comprehensive evil, because he is quite limited; indeed, he has been invented by his victim, and falls soon after his victim ceases to hate his own invention" (pp. 97–98).

5. Stuart Curran, *Shelley's Annus Mirabilis*, p. 123.

6. As Earl Wasserman suggests, Shelley might well have regarded psychiatry as antithetical to poetry. "Self-anatomy . . . is the introversion of the individual mind in order to examine all that is deposited there by experience, and it results in the mind's becoming adjusted and reconciled to what it finds. Shelley's stoicism is in exact contradiction to all theories that psychoanalysis is carthartic" (*Shelley: A Critical Reading* (Baltimore, 1971), p. 111). However, where Wasserman here sees stoicism as the means of personal control, I will argue in this chapter that the indirections of poetry fulfill that role for Shelley.

7. Milton Wilson condenses the list of *self* and its compounds in *The Shelley Concordance*, and finds that of 27 substantive entries, "by far the largest number of entries (nine) is under *self-contempt*, to which might be added those under headings like *self-mistrust* and *self-despising*. About half these entries are from *Prometheus Unbound*." *Shelley's Later Poetry: A Study of His Prophetic Imagination* (New York, 1959), pp. 145–50.

8. Milton Wilson, *Shelley's Later Poetry*, pp. 63–64; Wasserman, *Shelley*, pp. 258–61.

9. G. M. Matthews, "A Volcano's Voice in Shelley," *ELH* 24 (1957), pp. 191–228; Wasserman, "The Breathing Earth," *Shelley*, pp. 326–58. Other accounts of imagery in *Prometheus Unbound* derived from the physical sciences are: Desmond King-Hele, "A Newton Among Chemists?" and "Prometheus Unbound," in *Shelley: His Thought and Work* (London, 1960), pp. 155–211, and Carl Grabo, *A Newton Among Poets: Shelley's Use of Science in Prometheus Unbound* (Chapel Hill, N.C., 1930).

10. Wasserman, *Shelley*, pp. 320–23.

11. *The Aeneid of Vergil*, trans. John Dryden, ed., with introduction and notes, Robert Fitzgerald (New York, 1964), p. 179.

12. Three hundred twenty lyrical lines: 513 narrative (total—833).

13. Two hundred twenty-four lyrical lines: 462 narrative (total—686).

14. Four hundred twenty-one lyrical lines: 157 narrative (total—578).

15. "Even William Michael Rossetti, perceiving the horrors of such an eternity, reluctantly admitted that Prometheus here comes perilously close to 'an idealized Leigh Hunt.'" Douglas Bush, *Mythology and the Romantic Tradition in English Poetry* (Cambridge, Mass., 1937), pp. 145–50).

16. *The Literary Criticism of William Wordsworth*, ed. Paul M. Zall (Lincoln, Nebr., 1966), p. 19.

17. Shelley's argument is derived from an Empirical understanding of time, which ultimately goes back to Locke. In Chapter XIV of the *Essay Concerning Human Understanding* (1690), "Idea of Duration and its Simple Modes," Locke says, ". . . we have our notion of succession and duration from this original, viz. from reflection on the train of ideas, which we find to appear one after another in our own minds . . . we have no perception of duration but by considering the train of ideas that take their turns in our understandings." In Shelley's adaptation, this allows for an expansion of time, through lyrical ecstasy—we prolong clock time by imaginatively increasing the pace and vividness of our passing impressions. Locke would not have allowed for this possibility. In the chapter on duration he remarks, "This appearance of [ideas] in train, though perhaps it may be sometimes faster and sometimes slower, yet, I guess, varies not very much in a waking man: there seem to be certain bounds to the quickness and slowness of the succession of those ideas one to another in our minds, beyond which they can neither delay nor hasten."

18. See text, p. 85.

19. Wasserman, *Shelley*, p. 373.

20. I am aware that there is a debate over whether Shelley intends millennium or apocalypse. In *Shelley's Later Poetry* Milton Wilson senses some degree of confusion in the poet's intentions; he speaks of *Prometheus Unbound* as "irresolute as well as unresolved. . . . Nevertheless, the poem has more tension than muddle, more direction than aimlessness" (p. 279). In *Shelley*, Wasserman replies by drawing a distinction between the transcendental and timeless existence of the One Mind and the temporal existence of human beings, and adding that in the apocalypse mankind "will no longer be man, the modified portion of the One Mind, but will be absorbed into the unity of Existence. . . . However, since man now [in Act IV of *Prometheus Unbound*] makes mutability his slave, his relation to time is thereby altered. . . . The two goals of time, then,

do not result from any confusion by Shelley of a millennium with an apocalypse . . . Shelley's apocalypse and millennium are the forms of perfection at the two different levels of Existence: the timelessness of the One Mind and the nearest possible approximation to that condition in the human mind, which subsists as human mind by virtue of the illusions of diversity and change" (p. 361). I wish to defer my own discussion of this issue to my chapter on *Epipsychidion*, where the question again arises, in a context where I am more fully prepared to deal with it.

CHAPTER FIVE

Transforming Love and Death: *Epipsychidion* and *Adonais*

Like *Prometheus Unbound*, Shelley's next major poems, *Epipsychidion* and *Adonais*, break new ground in his quest to expand the scope of lyricism. Wasserman's important reading of *Adonais* has identified a cardinal feature of this poetry—that in order to achieve resolution it moves through a series of changing world-hypotheses.[1] Or, as I would say, this is a poetry of transformation. However, my view of Shelleyan transformation does not include the poetic literalism that creeps into Wasserman's account. His language tends to suggest that *Adonais* is a philosophical search for truth and that the poem itself is the searcher—a kind of impersonal world-mind that is writing itself. For instance, he says that "the materials of the poem . . . drive forward through three successive tableaux, each being fashioned by the redistribution of the unstably ordered materials of the previous tableau; and each of the self-generated redistributions rejects the previous hy-

pothesis";[2] and even more explicitly, "the poem will complete
itself artistically only when these latent factors have expended
their shaping energy."[3] Consequently, he can speak of the poem's
"successive hypotheses" and its nearing approximation to "prob-
able truths." For him *Adonais* becomes a configuration of images
which work toward "the most nearly perfect order of which they
are capable."[4]

But this configuration of images exists in a singer's mind, and
the transformations in its order are due to the singer's changing
way of looking at the world. Far from being an impersonal search
for truth, *Epipsychidion* and *Adonais* express the experiences of
persons who find themselves in the process of fundamental
change. Like *Prometheus Unbound*, *Epipsychidion* and *Adonais* are
lyrics of personal transformation. And the technique of these
poems exhibits a significant relationship to Shelley's "Lyrical
Drama": in fact, they could be termed dramatic lyrics. Where
Prometheus Unbound is the drama of a world in the process of
lyrical transformation, *Epipsychidion* and *Adonais* are the lyric expressions of individuals experiencing the drama of personal
transformation. Viewed in this way, the poems become prominent early examples of an important nineteenth-century mode that
Robert Langbaum calls "the poetry of experience."[5] Shelley's
special version of this poetry of experience is a poetry of ideal
experience: he shows us ideal episodes of self-development, transformations in which the human strives towards the divine.

Of course, the poet cannot literally become a divinity, but he
can create a poem that articulates his ideal. The "I," or singer, of
his poem becomes the living poet's other self, his mirror, his
indirect way of addressing himself; and this persona is a form
which allows for personal transformation. Through poetry
Shelley becomes both his own divinity and its worshipper. In the
heaven of the poetry, ideal form takes shape in the experience of
the lyrical "I"; and on the earth, the realm of the writer and his

readers, a love of that evolving perfection and a desire to approximate its forms sparks the improvement of life. In heaven there is perfection; on earth there is perfectibilism.[6]

But if there is a division implied between the heaven of poetry and the earth of our life in these poems, the realms are different only in kind, not in quality. Like earth, heaven is involved in ongoing experience rather than finality. It too undergoes constant change, movement, transformation. In fact, when heaven ceases to move, it also ceases to exist—and that is exactly what happens at the conclusion of both *Epipsychidion* and *Adonais*, when the experience of perfection goes as far as it can be carried and the lyricist has to cease singing his world. He stops not because he has failed but because he has completely succeeded. The ideal of the poem has been so far attained that there is no more room for movement, and in the final rapture of universal fusion his world passes beyond existence. This, however, does not amount to an apocalypse, a translation into some transcendental realm. Rather, the Shelleyan poem simply dies of its own happiness. Then the only way to renew life will be to begin writing a new poem.

Shelley's mature poetry implies a lyrical idealism that must never cease creating itself, both transformationally within the poems themselves, and in the movement from poem to poem. Existence implies experience, which is quintessentially movement. The Shelley of 1821 has come a long way from *Alastor*, his first effective poem of movement: like *Alastor*, *Epipsychidion* and *Adonais* turn upon the separation of the lover from his beloved (Emily, Adonais); but where the *Alastor* Poet moved silently through a static world in the futile search for a real person who would correspond to his ideal vision, the "I" of *Epipsychidion* and *Adonais*, himself a transformational projection of Percy Bysshe Shelley, sings out a poetic world that transforms repeatedly, until it becomes the heaven in which the beloved ideal can appear. At that point, it suddenly becomes apparent that the "I" himself has been changed into what he has sought. Like Asia in Act II of

Prometheus Unbound, the maker of the poem discovers that he has been indirectly transformed by his own poetic activity.

Epipsychidion

Epipsychidion is composed of three transformational sections. The first section is the poem's first 189 lines, which expound the poet's ideas of free love and haltingly attempt to act upon them; the second runs from lines 190 through 287 and comprises the history of his youth, which very much resembles the narrative of *Alastor* but ends in a quite different way; and the last extends from lines 288 through 591 and involves creation of the poem's heaven.

In the first section the singer, whose "name my heart lent to another" (46), speaks for love, which like imagination, should be essentially free and various:

> Love is like understanding, that grows bright,
> Gazing on many truths; 'tis like thy light,
> Imagination! which from earth and sky,
> And from the depths of human fantasy,
> As from a thousand prisms and mirrors, fills
> The Universe with glorious beams, and kills
> Error, the worm, with many a sun-like arrow
> Of its reverberated lightning. Narrow
> The heart that loves, the brain that contemplates,
> The life that wears, the spirit that creates
> One object, and one form, and builds thereby
> A sepulchre for its eternity.
>
> (163–73)

From the first, then, love and imagination are crucially related. By limiting themselves to "One object, and one form," as the *Alastor* Poet did, they lose their vitality and truth. Imagination should abandon itself to the luxuriance of "a thousand prisms and mirrors"; for instead of creating confusion, these multiple views will "fill/ The Universe with glorious beams, and kill/ Error." Likewise, love, "like understanding . . . grows bright,/ Gazing on many truths"; that is, by loving many objects. Both love and imagination are enthusiastic phenomena for Shelley, and so what his narrator is speaking for here is related to the enthusiastic creativity expressed in Act IV of *Prometheus Unbound*. There, energy supplied its own self-control—unrestrained expressiveness produced not chaos but a divinely transformed world. The hope of *Epipsychidion* is for a similar total release of energy, which should produce a similar paradise.

But this promise is not fulfilled in the first section. Instead of lyrical power, the poet is capable only of lyrical stridency; instead of creating a thousand coordinated prisms of metaphor, he creates an abundance of unrelated figures. The poetry becomes a chaos of roses, birds, Moons, fountains, lutes, stars, Spouses, and so on. The fragments do not yield a whole vision. However, although such a judgment has been made about these passages of *Epipsychidion*, the failure generally has been charged to Shelley's account.[7] Actually it belongs to his fictional poet: the poem is a dramatic performance, and Shelley, through his singer, is enacting a certain kind of poetic failure.

Consider the opening exclamations of the poem's first few paragraphs. This is the series: "Sweet spirit!" (1) . . . "Poor captive bird!" (2) . . . "High, spirit-wingèd Heart!" (3) . . . "Seraph of Heaven!" (4) . . . "Sweet Lamp!" (6). These metaphors describe Emily; and although in themselves they do not create a stable metaphorical system, understood as a dynamic configuration, they do suggest a wildly uncontrolled upward flight. Emily begins as a caged bird, beating her "unfeeling bars with vain endeavor" (14) but soon is transformed into more spirit than bird, then more seraph than spirit, then more beaconing lamp than seraph. In the first 50 lines of the poem the singer's metaphorical prolixity has managed to free Emily from her earthly imprisonment by dematerializing her and allowing her to ascend into the realm of high spirituality. However, within these same lines the poet himself is pulled downward, into an exhaustion that is quite understandable considering his shrill lyrical exertions. The risen Emily becomes a "Sweet lamp" luring his "moth-like Muse," which "burns[s] its wings" (53). He fearfully exclaims, "What have I dared? Where am I lifted? how/ Shall I descend, and perish not?" (124–25). As Emily becomes higher and more spiritual, her poet sees himself becoming lower and increasingly burdened with "much mortality and wrong" (36); his lyrical efforts to reach her become presumptuous and even dangerous to his life.

This situation is a variant of the *Alastor* archetype. The ideal and the real, the beloved and the lover, are parted absolutely, because they are seen as inhabiting different worlds. However, the poet of *Epipsychidion* himself has created these two worlds by his own inadvertent use of language. He is a poet not in control of his own material—all the while that he wildly generates metaphors which do not coalesce into the kind of world he wills, the subterranean implications of his language form a division of worlds that he does not want. This formation is not simply accidental, for it expresses the way that he fears things really are. It seems, then, that his declarations about the freedom of the sovereign imagination are propositions he himself does not really quite believe in.

His dissatisfaction with his own poetry suggests that this analysis is correct. He says his song is only "dim words, which obscure" Emily (33); his "names, though dear, could paint not, as is due,/ How beyond refuge I am thine" (50–51), and he "measure[s]/ The world of fancies, seeking one like thee,/ And find[s] —alas! mine own infirmity" (69–71). These statements implicitly deny that the imagination can create its own proper world; for in each of them Emily is a reality which stands outside language and only can be reflected in it.[8] The corollary is that the poet never possibly can achieve union with her through his song; and of course, that is the outcome of the first section. The climactic description of Emily which the singer's struggling flight of meta-

phor has been building toward in section one betrays this lin-
guistic infirmity:

> See where she stands! a mortal shape indued
> With love and life and light and deity,
> And motion which may change but cannot die;
> An image of some bright Eternity;
> A shadow of some golden dream; a Splendour
> Leaving the third sphere pilotless; a tender
> Reflection of the eternal Moon of love
> Under whose motions life's dull billows move;
> A Metaphor of Spring and Youth and Morning;
> A vision like incarnate April, warning,
> With smiles and tears, Frost the Anatomy
> Into his summer grave.
>
> (112–23)

Emily is present, and yet not present, in this rapturous description. "She stands" there, but she is so much more than her poet
can say—his described Emily is an "image," a "shadow," a
"Reflection," a "Metaphor," a "Vision," of something existing
beyond his verbal powers. He cannot touch her because his poetry
essentially has been unable to conceive of what she is. It seems,
then, that Emily is a sort of *Ding an sich* that cannot be grasped by
the world of the imagination. This view is the real source of the
poet's lyrical weakness, for if it is true, then all poetry, not only
his own, is inherently weak—is a world of words without the
power to engage reality.

But the death of the poem's first section is not the death of
Epipsychidion itself. Instead of ceasing, the singer begins another
kind of song. To understand why, once more consider this passage from the *Defence*: "Poetry enlarges the circumference of the
imagination by replenishing it with thoughts of ever new delight,
which have the power of attracting and assimilating to their own
nature all other thoughts, and which form new intervals and
interstices whose void forever craves fresh food" (VII, 118).[9] For

Shelley, song is like an expanding circle, a sovereign creation
of space that radiates around the singer and extends to his horizons. The fabric of this circle is bound to develop "intervals" and
"interstices," and their "void" will "crave fresh food." That
food is a transformation in the singing, an attempt at something
new which might fill the gaps in the singer's sense of things—
make his world complete. The Shelleyan lyric always moves
toward closure, but as this passage from the *Defence* suggests, new
gaps always will tend to open in its fabric. This means that the
song must continue moving for as long as it exists, pursuing a
closure that it never quite attains.

So in *Epipsychidion*, the imagination necessarily expands because
of the inadequacies of its own activity. The poetry of the first
section has created "new intervals and interstices whose void
forever craves fresh food." The lyrical flight, which has arisen
from a void, mounts up only to encounter another void. But this
is not a circular movement, for the new void is transformed in
character by the activity which has revealed it. In this case,
although the singer's poetry has failed to unite him with Emily, it
has revealed the inadequacy of a conception of poetry as simple
lyrical flight directly attempting to grasp its objects of desire.

Because sheer lyricism has not served him well enough, in the
second section the poet transforms his material by embodying it
in another literary form—the autobiographical narrative. From
this new perspective we can identify part of the problem with his
lyricism: the start of *Epipsychidion* sounded shrill because it burst
into existence on the kind of high note that one usually associates
with climaxes, not beginnings. One good reason that it inhabited
a void, then, was because it had no solid place from which to
start. So in the second section, the poet attempts to establish a
beginning by telling the story of his life. This is to the point, for if
as a poetic form the lyric aims at expressing the essential self in a
transcendent outpouring of song, the autobiographical narrative
has a related function: to explain the essential self by describing

how it has grown to be what it is. Autobiography will offer this singer a poetic resource not available through the first section lyric form—the temporal dimension. Instead of dwelling in a world of frantic immediacy, he will have time for the ordering possibilities of growth.

Here, comparing *Epipsychidion* to *The Prelude* can be enlightening. As Wordsworth said in the Preface to the *Lyrical Ballads*, for him poetry ideally was "the spontaneous overflow of powerful feelings," but feelings "recollected in tranquillity." When we recollect our feelings under the condition of tranquillity, "The emotion is contemplated till by a species of reaction the tranquillity gradually disappears, and an emotion, similar to that which was before the subject of contemplation, is gradually produced, and does itself actually exist in the mind. In this mood successful composition generally begins, and in a mood similar to this it is carried on. . . ."[10] This passage implies that poetry is transformed feeling, since the poetic emotion is "similar" to but not identical with the emotion elicited by the poet's original experience. By itself a spontaneous overflow of feeling is not poetry; it requires the addition of a temporal and meditative dimension—recollection in tranquillity—to transform the raw materials of life into imaginative form. Thus, *The Prelude*; and also the first two sections of *Epipsychidion*, where Shelley at first offers a dramatic impression of his poet experiencing a "spontaneous overflow of powerful feelings," which by its failure of self-sufficiency demonstrates the need for the subsequent recollection in tranquillity of the second section. In this sense, the subject matter of this section actually is the same as that of the first; the difference is that it is considered within the perspective of a different kind of poetic form. And if form is emerging as the prime concern of *Epipsychidion*, then we must pay particular attention to the way in which the singer formulates his life. Although his autobiography is the old *Alastor* story of a youth who wanders through the world seeking the prototype of his own conception, the sameness of this archetype becomes less important than the differences in its imaginative formulation.

In *Alastor* the narrator notes the Poet's postvisionary world of "clear and garish hills,/ . . . distinct valley and . . . vacant woods" that is reflected in the emptiness of the Poet's own "wan eyes" which "Gaze on the empty scene as vacantly/ As ocean's moon looks on the moon in heaven" (194–95, 200–2). The void that opens in this poem is the void of depressive blankness, not the void of transformational change. The *Alastor* Poet never will change because he cannot change his way of seeing. Of course, this imaginative singlemindedness is caused by his singlemindedness in love. He believes in objectively existing love and truth, and therefore the problem of formulation never arises: it does not occur to him that the objects one sees may be conditioned by one's way of seeing.

At first glance the autobiographical narrative of *Epipsychidion* also may suggest a speaker who believes in objectivity; for in the beginning it assumes the form of allegory, a formulative method that can be used to clothe transcendental truth in sensuous appearance. This is the method of the *Faerie Queene* and Dante's *Vita Nuova* and *Divine Comedy*, which do provide models for Shelley's poem.[11] Certainly some of the autobiographer's details encourage an allegorical reading: forsaken by the "veiled Divinity" of his youth, he wanders

> Into the wintry forest of our life;
> And struggling through its error with vain strife,
> And stumbling in my weakness and my haste,
> And half bewildered by new forms, I passed,
> Seeking among those untaught foresters
> If I could find one form resembling hers,
> In which she might have masked herself from me.
> (249–55)

But this speaker's world turns out not to be the world of Fidessa
and Duessa, and certainly not of Una. As the autobiography
continues, what begins to emerge is not the single truth behind
appearances but the formulated appearance of truth. The temporal
dimension of this narrative, which allows for growth, does not
work back to a One Truth beyond language, but forward, to a
truth that evolves from the speaker's expressions. The poet's
personal growth is conveyed through a language that itself grows;
what begins as allegory and illustrative metaphor, detachable
from the real story it embellishes, coalesces into a comprehensive
figurative language that creates a world inseparable from its own
mode of expression. Appropriately, the culminating image of this
world is itself a world: Shelley's lovers become a solar system.

   This process of language growth can be noted in the poet's
treatment of his Moon and Sun, which begin their lives as allegorical representations of women he has loved:

> One stood on my path who seemed
> As like the glorious shape which I had dreamed
> As is the Moon, whose changes ever run
> Into themselves, to the eternal Sun
>
> (277–80)

And Emily comes

> Soft as an Incarnation of the Sun,
> When light is changed to love
>
> (334–35)

This Moon and Sun come into existence as allegory formulated in
the language of metaphor. But once the metaphors are intro-
duced into the narrative, they gain a life of their own which
begins to transform the narrator's speech. When he is able to see
himself as "This world of love" (346), the accumulating cosmological appearances have transformed themselves from mere
comparisons into a cosmos in which the speaker becomes an Earth

surrounded by a Moon, a Sun, and a Comet. As in Act IV of
Prometheus Unbound, the gravitational interaction of these celestial
bodies creates a world made coherent and self-perpetuating, so
that its principle of order is immanent.

Just as the content of this vision suggests an immanent dynamic, so also its formulation has been by a process of imma-
nence. The world-image simply emerged from appearances; it is
not a revelation of some underlying truth that exerts an exterior
force upon the poet's language. His vision is a configuration of
appearance, a contextual scheme. As in the "Hymn to Intellectual
Beauty," the fragmentary and decorative metaphors have co-
alesced into a comprehensive vision which transforms them,
giving them a new meaning inseparable from their new context.[12]
The increasingly sophisticated poet of the second section begins
to understand this contextual property of his language, which is
artistic because it arranges the appearances. He does not take the
revelations of his language literally, as he had attempted to do in
the first section. Not for a moment does he think he actually is a
world, or that his loves actually are a moon and a sun; but he does
use the appearances, for they give him a means to express what
otherwise would be unsayable. He begins to realize that truth is
not detachable from its manner of expression; and that conversely,
one's mode of expression actually can create truths.

Here Shelley's differences from Wordsworth are as interesting as ~~Sh + Ww~~
his resemblances. Where both believe in the self-expressive potential of autobiography, Shelley deals in a more radically
imaginary kind of autobiography. For him, the artistic transformation of experience comes not from recalling the real scenes and
landscapes of childhood, but from dwelling within a world of
words—that is, within an already poetic world—and transforming those words into a form expressing his individual sensibility.
In this light we can see that the comparisons of Emily to "Thou
Moon beyond the clouds!," "Thou Star above the Storm!," and

"Thou Mirror/ . . . the splendour of the Sun" (27–31) tossed out in the lyrical flight of the first section are not only fragmentary there, but also are merely the conventional complementary formulas of love poetry. The autobiographical poet of the second section has transformed these banalities by visualizing them within his own context, so that Emily's existence as a Sun becomes part of an original poetic cosmos.

He has created a world in which love is inseparable from imagination: now we can see that love's intuitions cannot become actualities until they achieve imaginative expression. But of course, the mode of this actual existence is imaginative. The speaker actually is not living with the "Sun," "Moon," and "Comet" by making a poetic world that includes them; instead, the actuality he attains is an actuality of self-expression, a way of formulating his feeling which allows him to recognize himself. In the first section he had made theoretical declarations in favor of free love and free imagination, but by reformulating this material through the poetic cosmos of the second section, he now can see much more clearly what he had meant: love and imagination need to be various and free, for only when they are liberated can they create a world that becomes coherent through its own internal dynamic. In a state of separation the speaker is a "Chaos" (243), not a world, the Comet is a destroyer, and the Moon so dominates existence that the whole world reflects only her chaste, cold calm. But the excesses of each solitary individual are balanced out, and even turned into virtues, through the integrating context of love.

In seeing all this the speaker is not unearthing a fact, he is making a poem. Expressing clearly what you meant turns out not to be a descriptive process but a fabricative one; and it points not toward a world of objective reality but a world that the singer hopes for and desires. In other words, poetic self-realization turns out to be a movement toward a personal ideal. This is evident from the imperative mode in which the last half of the planet-world passage is expressed. The first part, lines 345 through 359, appears to be in the present tense ("Twin Spheres of light who rule this passive Earth/ This world of love, this *me* . . ."), but after a while this present tense evolves into an imperative that looks toward an idealized future ("So ye, bright regents, with alternate sway/ Govern my sphere of being, night and day!").

How different this concluding mode is from the ending of the first section! There, the narrator's naive lyricism was accompanied by the naive expectation that perhaps he could rise through his poetry actually to embrace Emily. In this belief, he resembles the literalistic *Alastor* Poet, who arose from his dream and actually stretched his arms out to embrace his vision. The imagination simply cannot make these kinds of transformations. What it can do, as it does in the second section, is to create its own world of love within which all objects may be embraced.

Given such imaginative triumph, it becomes important to ask why the poem does not simply end here. Newman Ivey White saw the necessity of raising this question. Assuming that *Epipsychidion* is Shelley's "spiritual autobiography," he felt that the poem should end with its vision of the speaker's life organized as a cosmos, for "The long imaginary elopement" which follows then strikes one as "an addition imperfectly welded to a poem already artistically and logically complete." [13] But this judgment ignores the poem's fundamental commitment to plurality. *Epipsychidion* is not simply Shelley's spiritual autobiography; rather, Shelley's spiritual autobiography is but one of its poet's means of formulating the various nature of love and imagination. The speaker presses toward yet another formulation in the third section of his poem, because the poetry of the second section does indeed leave something to be desired.

Although his cosmic image has been very largely effective, it does posit a problem of "coolness" or distance. In one way the poet's ability to stand apart from his creation, to recognize its imaginary nature, is a virtue because this attitude protects him from the dangers of naive literalism. But in exchange for that protection he has forfeited the ecstatic expectations with which the poem began. In the first section the poet had said of Emily, "I am not thine: I am a part of *thee*" (52); although this rapturous singer then created a poetic shambles, his failure had in it an all-out commitment of energy, a total devotion to his cause, that is not matched in the cooler and more organized narrative of the second section.

The poet's cosmological imagery itself betrays this. In this imaginary solar system he is supported by the "Twin Spheres of light who rule this passive Earth" (345), suggesting that he is a recipient rather than a producer of energies. That this way of taking his image is not dictated by its internal logic but by the development of the poem in which it appears can be seen clearly by comparing this particular imagery to the cosmological imagery in Act IV of *Prometheus Unbound*. There the Sun's and Moon's dance creates a perfect gravitational balance: the power that penetrates each planet-lover's heart is complemented by the energies that burst forth to in turn penetrate the beloved. Clearly, this reciprocity is more in line with the actual dynamic of gravitation than is the metaphorical imbalance of energies depicted in *Epipsychidion*.

This differing treatment of the planetary scheme in *Prometheus Unbound* and *Epipsychidion* is explained largely by the point at which they occur as parts within the organic development of the whole poems which contain them. The dance of the planets in *Prometheus Unbound* concludes the play and enacts the imagination's total penetration and transformation of the world's body. In this figure, matter becomes spiritualized, attains self-consciousness and the power of poetic expression. Here is the triumph of complete integration: spirit and body become not separate elements but an identity. Each becomes a necessary aspect of the other, so that the universe is seen as a fusion of opposites which creates an organic whole. Like *Prometheus Unbound*, the whole of

Epipsychidion evolves toward a rapturously fusive conclusion. So
the cosmological imagery that occurs in the middle of the poem is
a necessary stage in the growth of its poet's mind because it links
the first section of the poem and the third section, the first impulse of poetic inspiration, which is a rapturous but disastrously
unmediated lyricism, and the fully developed power of poetic
creation, which is a sophisticated but nevertheless fully enthusiastic and fusive lyricism. Imagination, as well as love, requires an
act of absolute union; and so the fully articulate poet must participate unreservedly in his own creation rather than standing apart
from it, as does the speaker who creates the cosmological image.
Here, Coleridge's famous distinction between allegory and symbol is relevant:

> Now an allegory is but a translation of abstract notions into a
> picture-language, which is itself nothing but an abstraction
> from objects of the senses; the principal being more worthless
> even than its phantom proxy, both alike unsubstantial, and
> the former shapeless to boot. On the other hand a symbol
> . . . is characterized by a translucence of the special in the
> individual, or of the general in the special, or of the universal
> in the general; above all by the translucence of the eternal
> through and in the temporal. It always partakes of the reality
> which it renders intelligible; and while it enunciates the
> whole, abides itself as a living part in that unity of which it is
> the representative.[14]

Viewed in Coleridge's terms, *Epipsychidion* enacts the poetic
evolution from allegory to symbolism. In midpassage the poet
of the second section has attained a degree of coherence and self-
expression by standing at a distance from his own cool creation,
but the full expressiveness both of himself and of his imagination's
world will be achieved only when he is able to realize the ideal
he had hoped for in the first section, the unrestrained release of his
love and his imagination. To perform this he needs some kind of
context, such as the cosmological imagery of *Prometheus Unbound*,

which will reconcile the opposites of unrestricted self-expression
and poetic self-control.

In other words, the central concern of *Epipsychidion* continues to
be the search for an adequate formulation of feeling. Therefore,
just as the poet of the second section transformed the lyrical form
of the first section into the new form of autobiographical narrative, the poet of the third section now will tranform that autobiographical narrative into the form of the Romantic nature lyric.
This lyric is significantly different from the lyricism of the first
section, one which began in and struggled with a void, because
the growth of the second section has been toward the sophisticated recognition of what constitutes the imagination's world.
Consequently, unlike the lyrical poet of the first section, the
singer of the third section does not dissipate his energies by the
impossible lyrical flight toward an Emily regarded as a *Ding an
sich*, a real presence existing outside the world of his poetry.
Instead, he feels Emily already to be at his side: "The day is come
and thou wilt fly with me" (388).

Their lyrical flight is to the country of the imagination, a
landscape infused with the soul of its maker. For just as one may
discover the prototype of one's conception in the beloved, one
also can discover it in nature. Consider Shelley's remarks from *On
Love*: "We dimly see within our intellectual nature a miniature as
it were of our entire self, yet deprived of all that we condemn or
despise, the ideal prototype of every thing excellent or lovely that
we are capable of conceiving as belonging to the nature of man
. . . a mirror whose surface reflects only the forms of purity and
brightness; a soul within our soul that describes a circle around its
proper paradise, which pain, and sorrow, and evil dare not over-
leap" (VII, 201–2). This description applies equally well to Emily
or to the singer's "far Eden of the purple East" (417), an island
suspended in a magic lyrical circle that repels "Famine or Blight,/
Pestilence, War and Earthquake" (461–62) and even "the wingèd
storms, chanting their thunder-psalm/ To other lands," which

"leave azure chasms of calm/ Over this isle" (465–67). Imagining an island paradise becomes yet another way of formulating the material that has been the subject matter of all three sections of the poem: the striving of the imagination to embody its ideal. This island supersedes the imaginary cosmos of the second section because it is an alternative world that finally provides the singer a context within which he may fulfill his desire. Because this last world of *Epipsychidion* resembles the natural world but is different from it because ideally transformed by the imagination, the singer also can see his physical presence there as that of an ordinary man but ideally transformed by the imagination.

Finally, then, imagination redeems not only the world's body but also the singer's. A retrospective glance suggests this is a transformation much needed by this poet. In the first section he was so burdened by his own sense of sin and of Emily's divinity that he could say of himself, "The spirit of the worm beneath the sod/ In love and worship, blends itself with God" (128–29). In the second section the worm became an Earth, which is no doubt an improvement, but nevertheless did involve the disadvantages of passivity and of distance between the singer and the objects of his desire. It seems, then, that in his poetic past this singer has suffered from both self-contempt and a lack of self-confidence.

But in the third section he becomes an ideal human being capable of creating what can be the ideal human action—the act of sex. This becomes the climax and death of his poem:

> And we will talk, until thought's melody
> Become too sweet for utterance, and it die
> In words, to live again in looks, which dart
> With thrilling tone into the voiceless heart,
> Harmonizing silence without a sound.
> Our breath shall intermix, our bosoms bound,
> And our veins beat together; and our lips
> With other eloquence than words, eclipse
> The soul that burns between them, and the wells

Which boil under our being's inmost cells,
The fountains of our deepest life, shall be
Confused in Passion's golden purity,
As mountain-springs under the morning sun.
We shall become the same, we shall be one
Spirit within two frames, oh! wherefore two?
One passion in twin-hearts, which grows and grew,
Till like two meteors of expanding flame,
Those spheres instinct with it become the same,
Touch, mingle, are transfigured; ever still
Burning, yet ever inconsumable:
Like flames too pure and light and unimbued
To nourish their bright lives with baser prey,
Which point to Heaven and cannot pass away:
One hope within two wills, one will beneath
Two overshadowing minds, one life, one death,
One Heaven, one Hell, one immortality,
And one annihilation. Woe is me!
The winged words on which my soul would pierce
Into the height of Love's rare Universe,
Are chains of lead around its flight of fire—
I pant, I sink, I tremble, I expire!

(560–91)

Here is the final formulation of *Epipsychidion*: the imagination of
ideal sexual union becomes the organic unity which incorporates
and transforms all the fragments of the singer's poem.[15] The
cosmological imagery of the second section is present in this
passage, as is the enthusiastic flight into chaos of the first section.
But the point is that these are not as they were: elements which
hitherto betrayed the failure or incompleteness of the poet's efforts
now are transformed by the new context into signs of power.
This singer has discovered a form which simultaneously allows
him uninhibited expression and poetic self-control, and imaginative love has found its most proper symbolism in the acts of the
body.

The surprise of the poem is that it was set in motion by an elusive transforming image, the divine reality of that Emily who was too glorious to be embraced by the poet's language—but it is ended by the mutual rapture of orgasm. This has been made possible by a progressive idealization of the poet's language, which creates images that progressively transform his body. He has come from worm to Earth to human being, and now, like Emily, he too is a divinity, his body the transforming image that absorbs and converts all the material of the poem.

If the divine sexuality of *Epipsychidion* is an ideal poetic achievement, nevertheless *A Discourse on the Manners of the Ancient Greeks Relative to the Subject of Love* makes clear that the artistic procedure of *Epipsychidion* accords with Shelley's opinions on the place of sexuality in actual life. The perfection of his poem is matched by his perfectibilist opinions:

> Man is in his wildest state a social being; a certain degree of civilization and refinement ever produces the want of sympathies still more intimate and complete; and the gratification of the senses is no longer all that is sought in sexual connection. It soon becomes a very small part of that profound and complicated sentiment which we call love, which is rather the universal thirst for a communion not merely of the senses but of our whole nature, intellectual, imaginative, and sensitive. . . . The sexual impulse, which is only one and often a small part of these claims, serves from its obvious and external nature as a kind of type or expression of the rest, as common basis, an acknowledged and visible link.[16]

In Shelley's view, sex should be the outgrowth of a long evolution of the inner life—for then it can become a "type or expression" of the whole personality, an "acknowledged and visible link" through the body to the world of spiritual communion. Under these conditions, the sexual body becomes a transforming image of the soul.

But as the end of *Epipsychidion* suggests, if ideal sexual climax

encompasses "one life," "One Heaven," and "one immortality,"
it also contains the Coleridgian opposites of "one death," "one
Hell," and "one annihilation." "Love's rare Universe" is the
climaxing creation of a moment, and the opposites it triumphantly embraces soon must fly apart again in disorder and
fragmentation. This is not surprising and should not be overly
dismaying, given the pluralistic environment of the poem.
Shelley's world simply is not Spenser's or Dante's; the stable order
possible for them through right relation to one God and one
truth is neither possible nor desirable for Shelley. Although the
sinking and expiring experienced by the poet as he completes his
song is the death of his poem as well as its climax, this does not
necessarily imply that *Epipsychidion* has failed to reach its own
proper goals. Within the boundaries of the poem itself, all is
transformationally fused, and there is no loss until the final in-
stant.

   It is only when we begin to look outside the poem's limits that
we sense loss. When the singer himself departs from his love's
world in the separate little poem of envoi to address "Marina,
Vanna, Primus, and the rest" (601), the other important persons
in his life, Shelley deliberately invokes a sense of incompleteness.
We see that these others simply cannot be guests in the singer's
world in the same way and at the same time as Emily. For
although *Epipsychidion* has been committed to diversity, it also has
been committed to contextual coherence, and that has made it
impossible for the poet to avoid at least successive unities of focus.
The poem has been one as well as many—it has isolated and
principally developed the singer's relationship with one person,
thereby creating one ideal era of self-development. The singer
poetically can conceive of such ideal episodes, but he cannot
conceive of an entire ideal life in which everything and everyone
could be properly related and nothing would be lost.

   Just as the poem itself has demonstrated the need for a proper context for sexuality, the stretches of life outside the poem suggested by the envoi in turn demonstrate the need for a proper context for poetry. Outside the boundaries of the poet's lyric, the powerful song that has built a world becomes "Weak Verses" which kneel at "your Sovereign's feet" (592), a personage not quite the Emily of the poem itself. Instead of coming together in an orgasmic apotheosis, the poet and the lady of the envoi merely will share the reading of *Epipsychidion*. Imagination, which within the poem has embraced the entire world and transformed its every form, comes up against its inevitable limits: in life, after all, the poet cannot embrace the lady. Once again he is faced with the frustration that initiated his song. But now the lovers do have their poem, and if it cannot offer the satisfactions possible in life, to the imaginative it certainly can offer satisfactions of a different order. The relation of such poetry to life does not necessarily involve compromise.[17] What the reader first needs, if he is to feel his proper satisfaction, is the same love of the imaginative life displayed by the writer of *Epipsychidion*. He also needs the poet's sophisticated ability to tolerate plurality; for just as the poem itself constantly is changing, the reader's response to it also must be flexible. The faith of the imaginative idealist must not be rigidly absolute or it will lose its contact with the conditions of life and result in either irrelevance or disillusionment—that was the story of the *Alastor* Poet.

One may object that such a way of relating poetry to life looks extremely tenuous and difficult; the only possible answer is yes, of course it is. Just as Shelleyan poetry demands constant creativity of the poet, it also demands constant creativity of the reader. Its orientation is relentlessly toward openness. With greater force than ever before, Shelley ends this poem with skepticism and a challenge to the reader also suggested by the questions that end "Mont Blanc" and "Ode to the West Wind," and the warning by Demogorgon that concludes *Prometheus Unbound*.[18]

As for the lyricist of *Epipsychidion*, in achieving his poem's ultimate success he also has decreed its death. His climactic transforming image itself exhibits the reason for this: if heaven is understood to be ecstatic experience, the ultimate rapture of the moment such as is felt in orgasm, then of course it cannot last. Neither the human body nor spirit can sustain such intensities. But to close oneself to rapturous experience simply because it carries its own destruction would be cowardice. That this lyricist's vision insists on openness suggests his bravery—he will surrender himself to his joy, live to the fullest of his capacity, no matter what that course of action may bring. If he must die, then he chooses to die of happiness.

In *Epipsychidion* Shelley pushes the logic of his lyricism to the intense point where its limits as well as its infinity are revealed. The world-song in Act IV of *Prometheus Unbound* does not move to this kind of rapturous self-extinction because it is not sung by an individual person. What we hear there is the ideal voice of civilization, which has sufficient energy to sustain and express rapture indefinitely. But the individual singer does not have such collective resources. His ideal expressiveness is limited by the biological conditions of his existence. Thus, to speak of the difference between "millenium" or "Utopia" in *Prometheus Unbound*, and "apocalypse" in *Epipsychidion* and *Adonais*, seems to me a misapplication of terminology—an attribution of ontological ends to a poetry that aims not at the revelation of ultimate truths about the world, but to the rich creation of experience.[19] More radically than ever before in Shelley's poetry, *Epipsychidion* demonstrates that to *sing* is to *be*: the poem shows a self being formulated, shows how existence can become a function of expression. In this light, the poem's commitment to formal plurality also can be seen as a commitment to the maximization of experience. If we die, then before that happens we should live to the fullest. The lyrical mode offers precisely that option—life expressed with the greatest possible intensity, life sacrificing prudence or longevity to the service of achieving rapture. In this sense, the defeat at the end of the poem is also a victory: no matter what happens to him, the lyricist has *lived*.[20] ✓

And what of Shelley the poet, the lyrical dramatist who has created the singer of *Epipsychidion*? Just as his projection of ideally maximized experience has encountered the inevitable limits of death, so the creator of the poem discovers that his fiction must come to an end. His envoi demonstrates his awareness that the world of *Epipsychidion* indeed is not coincident with the actual world, which is too large and various to be comprehended as a whole by any one act of the imagination, no matter how hero- ically intense. Therefore, the finish of each of his poems will call for the creation of a new one; for like the lyricist of *Epipsychidion*, he must express himself in order to continue his imaginative life. Like the singer of "The Cloud," who nourishes the earth with his "fresh showers" and then destroys his creation by wielding "the flail of the lashing hail," the Shelleyan lyricist must bring his poetic worlds to their inevitable conclusions and then, to preserve the life of the imagination, move on to the creation of new songs. Only then can he say with the Cloud, "I change but I cannot die."

Adonais

Like *Epipsychidion*, *Adonais* consists of three transformational sections: stanzas I through XVII, in which the mourning poet sees the entire world as a decaying material hulk; stanzas XVIII through XXXV, in which the world seems to him split into the eternally self sustaining cycle of natural process and its opposite, the finite linear career of the human spirit; and stanzas XXXVI through LV, in which the world is again seen whole, this time as a material body capable of redemption by the imagination.

Although Wasserman gives a similar structural description of the poem, his emphasis upon the configuration of images in

Adonais, which he sees striving toward the "most nearly perfect order of which they are capable," creates the impression that the poem is writing itself. But the various world-views expressed in *Adonais* come from a completely interested and personal viewpoint: the perspective of the poem's speaker, who in contemplating his dead comrade's body, repeatedly sees the entire world transformed into the image of that body—a transformation which becomes at once a statement of the human condition and a forecast of his own future.

Shelley finds precedent for this fascination with the corpse in one of the two classical pastoral elegies he used as models for his poem, Bion's "Lament for Adonis." That poem luxuriates in the death of Adonis, again and again showing how "round his navel was floating dark blood: crimson from his thighs grew his chest, and purple beneath it Adonis' breasts that once were snowy," and granting "Adonis, a dead body now," the bed of his goddess lover because "Fair even in death is he . . . Lay him down in the soft coverlets wherein he used to rest when through the night he wrought with thee in holy sleep."[21] In section one of *Adonais* this eroticism of death is transformed by Shelley into a horror of death and of dead bodies. By a principle of antipathy the corpse becomes the focal point of the speaker's world, which against his wishes invades everything he sees and transforms all into images of deathliness. Although this is an inversion of the last world of *Epipsychidion*, where the lovers' bodies become the sympathetic "type and expression" of a world of ideal love, the governing principle of the two poems is the same: man's perception of his world depends upon possible transformational relationships between the human body and the world's body.

The dead Adonais was not only a human being but also a poet, as is the speaker who mourns him. Therefore another body, the body of poetry, enters into the symbolic complex of *Adonais*. In this connection, Shelley transforms the myth of Venus and Adonis that figures in the classical elegies which are his poetic models.

The goddess who mourns his Adonais becomes the dead poet's
mother rather than his lover, and her name becomes Urania rather
than Venus because she is the muse of poetry. That her transformation from lover to mother is related to her identification with
poetry is a revealing clue to the speaker's general idea of the poetic
enterprise. In section one of *Adonais* the body of poetry is seen as
ideally being a kind of protection, a deserved parental nurturing,
for young poets—who, unlike the imaginative lover of *Epipsychidion*, presumably are not yet ready to assume adult roles. The
reproachful speaker asks Urania, "Where wert thou, mighty
Mother, when he lay . . . pierced by the shaft which flies/ In
darkness?" (9–11). This is the answer he imagines:

> With veilèd eyes,
> 'Mid listening Echoes, in her Paradise
> She sate, while one, with soft enamoured breath,
> Rekindled all the fading melodies,
> With which, like flowers that mock the corse beneath,
> He had adorned and hid the coming bulk of Death.
>
> (13–18)

Unlike the island paradise in *Epipsychidion*, which is the imagination's bold and sophisticated transformation of reality, Urania's
Paradise is a refuge from reality, a poetical retreat wherein the
Mother herself is mothered by the false consolations of a decorative poetry. The songs of this Paradise are "like flowers that mock
the corse beneath," for they "adorned and hid the coming bulk
of Death."

Apparently, then, at this level poetry is an ornate creation of
surfaces—a verbal cosmetic designed to conceal horror. Once we
see this, it becomes evident that section one of *Adonais* is just
that kind of poem. The elaborate pathetic fallacy of this section—
nature's fulsome weeping and mourning—what does it accom-
plish but to delay the inevitable moment when death must be
recognized? The poet invites us to Adonais' bier because we must

see the body "while still/ He lies, as if in dewy sleep he lay" (60–61), as though the false appearance of life were a consolation. Morning's tears "Dimmed the aëreal eyes that kindle day" (123), and "Grief made the young Spring wild, and she threw down/ Her kindling buds, as if she Autumn were" (136–37), paralyzing time, with the ambivalent result that Adonais' corpse remains freshly preserved but completely lifeless. The temporal texture of section one suggests that poetry creates a false eternity or paradise which we cling to for agonizing comfort as long as we possibly can.

But our grasp inevitably must fail; for ornate poetic formulas are an unsatisfactory substitute for the true body of poetry, which for the speaker of section one is the body of the poet himself. This becomes clear when Adonais' Splendours, "The quick Dreams,/ The passion-wingèd Ministers of thought,/ Who were his flocks" (73–75), pay a memorial visit to his bier. Shelley's friend John Taafe pointed out in his annotations of *Adonais* that the term "Splendour" comes from Dante and signifies "any kind of immaterial substance." [22] These Splendours surround the body, and as one kneels to kiss its mouth, "the damp death/ Quenched its caress upon his icy lips," making the Splendour "pass to its eclipse" (104–8). The spiritual fire of the poet's creation is absorbed by the damp body of his death, suggesting that the life of poetry can last only as long as the life of its poet. [23] This explains why time has stopped in section one of *Adonais*: the speaker, himself a poet, grieves not only for Adonais' death but also for his own. He creates an artificial poetic eternity not only to preserve Adonais' corpse, but to prolong his own life and song. But he achieves this result at the cost of sorrow. His lyric world necessarily must be an eternity of grief, forever paralyzed by the sense of his past loss and the dread of his future death.

Just as the uncontrolled lyric flight in the first section of *Epipsychidion* involved the creation of a void which destroyed the singer's efforts and forced him to transform his song into another

form, so also this ambivalent poetic eternity of *Adonais* at length
must disintegrate, compelling this poet to seek new consolations.
In *Adonais*, the simple progression of natural time accomplishes
this. At the beginning of section two we find that "Winter is come
and gone,/ But grief returns with the revolving year" (154–55).
Presumably then, a year has passed since the grieving Spring of
section one threw down her buds; although the poet still stands
by Adonais' bier, by this time the corpse has been decently
interred and the earth over it is covered with new flowers.

As the poet knows, this yearly natural cycle, which grants
Adonais a rebirth in the form of the flowers on his grave, would
comprise such poetic consolation as seems possible for the classical
elegist whose form he is following. In Bion's "Lament for
Adonis," Cytherea's tears mingle with Adonis' blood and both
"are turned to flowers; of the blood are roses born, and of the
tears anemones." But the poem's last statement is, "Cease thy
laments, today Cytherea; stay thy dirges. Again must thou lament, again must thou weep another year." The elegy so ends
because this kind of transformation—man into flower—offers not
so much the consolations of immortality as the eternally recurring memory of grief. Although the flower may remind Cytherea
of her slain lover, the flower is not itself the man, and indeed,
serves only to vividly recall her loss.

So the cyclical resolution of the classical elegy is not really very
different from the artificial poetic eternity of *Adonais'* section
one. Although the one is an unnatural prolongation of time and
the other is a submission to the seasonal recurrences of natural
time, both serve to perpetuate grief: one kind of time preserves a
corpse and the other kind creates a memorial flower, but neither
can re-create the lost unique human being. As Moschus says, in
his "Lament for Bion": "Alas, when in the garden wither the
mallows, the green celery, and the luxuriant curled anise, they live
again thereafter and spring up another year, but we men, we that
are tall and strong, we that are wise, when once we die, unhearing

sleep in the hollow earth, a long sleep without end or waken-
ing." In section two of *Adonais* the speaker concurs with
Moschus. Himself bathed in the vitality of spring, he sees that
Adonais' "leprous corpse, touched by this spirit tender,/ Exhales
itself in flowers of gentle breath" (172–73). Such exhalation pointedly is not the breath of the man's life. The organic tenderness of
spring produces the loves and births of cyclical vitality, but this
creation is based upon the previous winter's deaths. The flowers
grow out of humus; their superficial beauty is nourished by the
deep horror of "The leprous corpse." Nature's creations in section
two are really not so different from poetry's creations in section
one: there the decorative veneer of poetry, "like flowers that mock
the corse beneath,/ . . . adorned and hid the coming bulk of
death"; here, actual flowers "illumine death/ And mock the merry
worm that wakes beneath" (175–76).

Just as the distinction between the eternal cycles of nature and
this artificial eternity of poetry turns out to be a distinction
without a real difference, so the Urania of section two, who is
unlike the paradise-dwelling Urania of section one because she
comes out into the world and is bound to natural time's cycle,
turns out to be a new Urania only insignificantly different from
the old. As she cries to her dead poet, "I would give/ All that I am
to be as thou now art!/ But I am chained to Time, and cannot
thence depart!" (232–34). Because she is chained to natural time,
this Urania tends to take a cyclical view of poetry. She thinks of
poets as timebound beings who attain full power only by developing through their "full cycle" and spiritually filling their
"crescent sphere" (241–42). There is a moment of optimum greatness for poetry, then, and that is during the mature phase of
poets' lives.

In describing the nature of this greatness, Urania draws upon
the part of the Venus and Adonis myth that portrays Adonis as an
unseasoned hunter killed by the boar he stalks. For her the poet's

art is analogous to the hunter's, and so Adonais was killed by prematurely daring "the unpastured dragon in his den" (238)—by speaking out freely before he had strength to cope with the inevitably ensuing attacks. Her best advice to the dead poet is that he should have exercised greater caution, should have restrained his blow, until his powers filled their "crescent sphere." The prudent preservation of life, rather than the creation of poetry, is Urania's first concern. This follows from her view of time, to which she is chained and from which she cannot depart. For if the natural cycle of life is all there is, then at any cost we must maximize the time nature grants us. This is a strategy doomed to ultimate failure, however, for the simple reason that eventually everyone must die. Like the paradise-enchanted Urania of section one, the prudent Urania of section two at best only can delay death for a time. Even her powerful mature poets, those capable of daring dragons, are "godlike mind[s]" soaring forth like the sun, "in [their] delight/ Making earth bare and veiling heaven," only to sink at last below the evening horizon, abandoning the living to "the spirit's awful night" (258–61). Because Urania knows that her poetry is an artifice that only temporarily delays the inevitable, her world is suffused with the same qualities of grief and dread as the world of section one. These poems do manage a kind of lyric life, but inevitably, it is a life of pain.

To this point, then, *Adonais* has created two worlds that turn out to offer distinctions bereft of real difference. At every turn the poet's maneuverings for a new vision, a new possibility of freedom, have been cancelled by the ubiquitous presence of death. He has envisioned two variations of nature, two Uranias, and two processions of mourners beside Adonais' bier—the Splendours in section one, and now the company of Adonais' fellow poets in section two. If the poem were to run true to its previous form, these new mourners should be an insignificant variation upon the previous group.

Instead, the poet here at last finds his opening to freedom. Somewhat apart from the other mourners he sees a "Stranger" (303) who turns out to be—himself. This self-portrait often has been considered a piece of unforgivably indulgent self-pity.[24] But if we place it within the context of the dramatic lyric, it becomes evident that this is a transforming image which permits self-examination. The image functions as do the transforming images of Jupiter and Christ encountered by Prometheus: it is the poet's self, but made into a stranger whom he must confront. It is clothed as a hunter and a devotee of Dionysus, whose animal is that "pardlike Spirit" the leopard, and whose followers carry the thyrsus, a "light spear topped with a cypress cone" (280, 291). Here is appropriate dress for section two of *Adonais*, in which poetic genius seems equivalent to the strength of life's prime, and the making of poetry involves the hunting of one's foes. But it seems that to be a hunter has deranged this particular poet. Like the frenzied followers of Dionysus, his passions have possessed him. He is like Actaeon; for having "gazed on Nature's naked loveliness" and been driven mad, he wanders "With feeble steps o'er the world's wilderness,/ And his own thoughts, along that rugged way,/ Pursued, like raging hounds, their father and their prey" (275–79). It is the story of the *Alastor* Poet again. This wandering "Stranger" is a stranger to himself because he is his own destroyer. At once, he plays the roles of pursuer and pursued, hunter and quarry.

This is the classic Shelleyan poetic pathology, and as in *Prometheus Unbound*, *Adonais* shows this condition to be rooted in unexamined aggressive impulses. When Prometheus cursed Jupiter he also indirectly cursed himself, creating his own proper world of hatred. Likewise, in hating the attackers of Adonais, this hunter-poet has created a world in which poetry is used aggressively, to overpower its detractors—at least that is the intention. But in fact, the poet's aggressions have overcome himself, leading to the weakness and depression evident everywhere in the first two worlds of *Adonais*. This Stranger's "ensanguined brow" bears marks "like Cain's or Christ's" (306), just as Prometheus became by turns the images of Jupiter and Christ, because both Prometheus and the poet of *Adonais* are at once the murderer and the murdered, the crucifier and the crucified—their bodies are the worlds within which their aggression is both meted out and suffered. The poet inhabits a world of death not really because of Adonais' death, but because he has been one "Who in another's fate . . . wept his own" (300). The attacks on Adonais' poetry have mattered less to him than the attacks on his own, and his response has been a rage that indirectly has polluted his soul.

In stanza XXXVII he abandons his attack upon the critics, leaving them to inhabit the worlds they create for themselves, which in his opinion, is a just and entirely ample punishment: "be thyself and know thyself to be!" Adonais' critic remains in the cyclical world of section two, a viper whose venom overflows "ever at thy season," creating a "Remorse and Self-contempt" which "shall cling to thee." The self-inflicted poisoning suffered by the poet of section two is left for the critic, while the poet himself goes on to better things. He copes with his aggression by transforming its energy into a new form. In the new poem he creates in section three of *Adonais*, the emotional power previously devoted to hatred and dread is converted into an expression of imaginative joy.

This is the turning point of *Adonais*. Hitherto, the transforming image dominating the poem has been the body of death; but by encountering himself as a stranger, the poet has discovered that this body of death was not Adonais but himself. It is "*We*" who "decay/ Like corpses in a charnel" (348) when we live a life of hatred. The surprise of *Epipsychidion* was that the real transforming image of the poem was not Emily but the divine sexual body of her poet; similarly, the surprise of *Adonais* is that the poet has

created his own world of death and therefore equally well could
create his own world of immortality. All this is within his power
because the world he sees is a transformation of his own image,
his own body. In section three of *Adonais* the poetic energies that
hitherto had been turned morbidly inward will be radiated outward by the changed poet. He is freed to live, to feel joy, to
sing.[25]

But his immortal world is not to be construed literally. After
all, *Adonais* is a poem of immortality written by an atheist; we
must be careful in specifying the nature of its affirmations.[26]
Shelley's remarks about death and immortality in the *Essay on
Christianity* provide clarification. This essay depicts Christ as a
poet who created a liberal imaginative vision of life and death to
counter the narrow view that "Men shall die and their bodies shall
rot under the ground. . . . There is a time when we shall neither
hear nor see, neither be heard or be seen by the multitude of
beings like ourselves by whom we have been so long surrounded. . . . It appears that we moulder to a heap of senseless dust, a
few worms that arise and perish like ourselves" (VI, 235). This
picture of the leprous corpse, so strikingly similar to the views of
the first two sections of *Adonais*, and like them, the product of a
"gloomy and cold imagination," is countered by Christ's poetic
vision of a future wherein "Another and a more extensive state of
being, rather than the complete extinction of being, will follow
from that mysterious change which we call death. . . . The unob-
scured irradiations from the fountain-fire of all goodness shall
reveal all that is mysterious and unintelligible until the mutual
communications of knowledge and of happiness throughout all
thinking natures constitute a harmony of good that never varies
and never ends. This is Heaven, when pain and evil cease, and
when the benignant principle unt[rammel]led and uncontrolled,
visits in the fulness of its power the universal frame of things"
(VI, 235–36). Shelley's reaction to these images (which, as we

shall see, anticipate the imagery of section three of *Adonais*) is of
great interest: "How delightful a picture even if it be not true!
How magnificent & illustrious is the conception which this bold
theory suggests to the contemplation, even if it be no more than
the imagination of some sublimest and most holy poet, who
impressed with the loveliness and majesty of his own nature, is
impatient and discontented, with the narrow limits which this
imperfect life and the dark grave have assigned for ever as his
melancholy portion" (VI, 236). Apparently, Shelley does not
quite cease to believe in the leprous corpse; instead, he denies it.
The limits of mortality are narrow, and he thinks it well to replace
them with the expansiveness of the imagination. If on the one
hand we know that death does set our limits, on the other, if we
have experienced imaginative joy, we know it to be equally true
that the human spirit can have its moments of infinity.

   Consequently, section three of *Adonais* aims at giving both the
singer and the reader the *experience* of imaginative expansiveness,
which will constitute the immortality of this poem. The poem
affirms not an objective truth, but an action—the act of imaginative creation. This explains why it is so much more moving than
"The Sensitive Plant," Shelley's other major poem about death,
which in the end expresses a wistful longing for immortality but
is unable to imaginatively release an experience of deathless joy
within the confines of the poem. As in *Epipsychidion*, *Adonais*
finally acts out a completely poetic reality rather than making an
impossible effort to reach some *Ding an sich* outside its own lyric
universe. Here is not God's Heaven but "an Heaven of Song"
(413). This self-created heaven can be ideal, for although it comes
from the poet it also expands beyond him. It is simultaneously
his own human creation and the immortal vision seen by his best
imaginative self. The whole of *Adonais* enacts an ideal episode of
self-development, beginning with the poet's fear of death and
ending with his joyous creation of an imaginative immortality.

He begins by imaginatively embracing the world's body:

> Who mourns for Adonais? Oh, come forth,
> Fond wretch! and know thyself and him aright.
> Clasp with thy panting soul the pendulous Earth;
> As from a centre, dart thy spirit's light
> Beyond all worlds, until its spacious might
> Satiate the void circumference
>
> (415–20)

This echoes the poet's questions in section one ("I weep for
Adonais . . . Where wert thou, mighty Mother?"); but instead of
calling for Urania's help, here in section three he abandons de-
pendence upon the goddess in order to become his own poet.
Consequently, Urania vanishes from the poem—she is an authority no longer needed. As this passage suggests, the paradise
created by this poet will not be the poetic retreat of section one,
but the everyday world of life and death, transformed, irradiated,
enlarged, into his own proper paradise. By clasping the earth he
transforms it into a radiating center that darts spiritual light into
the "void circumference," creating the fulfilled sphere of the
imagination, the sovereign circle of the lyric. Like the island
paradise of *Epipsychidion*, this is a realm in which the world and
the human body remain themselves, but through imaginative
redemption exhibit their ideal potential.

When he releases this world-creating joy the singer at last can
see through the deathly "shadow of our night" (352) that hitherto
has dominated his perceptions; without denying the presence of
night, he sees that the black "void circumference" is irradiated by
stars. To the redeemed imagination, each of these is a projective
"centre," a testament of poetry. It is here that Adonais legit-
imately belongs, in a cluster inhabited by "the inheritors of
unfulfilled renown" (397)—Chatterton, Sidney, Lucan—poets
who died, as Urania would have said, before their "crescent

sphere" was filled. As Shelley's translation of his epigraph from Plato runs,

> Thou wert the morning star among the living,
>   Ere thy fair light had fled;—
> Now, having died, thou art as Hesperus, giving
>   New splendour to the dead.

Adonais, the fading morning star, is one and the same as Adonais, the emerging star of evening. Here the cyclical universe of section two falls away to reveal eternity, which is a moment of poetic truth disclosed in the perception of its singer. The lyricist sees that Urania was wrong in believing that poets should remain prudently silent until their maturity. Age is irrelevant; the mission of the poet is fearlessly to sing of eternity whenever he sees it. Because this poet now does so, he can cease to mourn the early death of Adonais. Adonais was a true singer, and so there is no reason to regret his passing. It is not the length of the poet's life that matters; it is the way in which it has been lived. Furthermore, if the dead have sung well in life, the living will take up their song and continue it, which happens here. In this final section of *Adonais* the dead poet is reborn in the song of the living one.

This transmission of the poetic tradition, another version of that "great poem" discussed in the *Defence*, "which all poets, like the co-operating thoughts of one great mind, have built up since the beginning of the world," is embodied in this poet's song by a striking image. He sees that the aggregate of heaven's poetic stars forms a "burning fountain" whose fire shoots downward to the earth's core and crests there, only to reverse direction and flow upward to its source, carrying along with it whatever "pure spirit" (338–39) it encounters in the earth. Such a fire-fountain inverts the vector of earth's water-fountains; it follows that its processes poetically reverse the processes of earth's mortal decay.[27] The poetic fire "Sweeps through the dull dense world" and resurfaces, in the process, "Torturing th' unwilling dross that checks its flight/ To its own likeness" (382, 384–85). Things that grow out of the earth—"trees and beasts and men" (387)—become forms which reveal the transformations of the upward-stressing poetic fire. The unity of this fiery "one Spirit" (381) is not neoplatonic or theistic; it is the oneness of the imagination—the transformational power of the world's poets, living and dead. Once again, Shelley's heaven emerges as the heaven of culture, the collective mind of civilization. But this is not an object with a real existence; it is a faith rekindled and transmitted through the song of the living.

Within this heaven of culture that embraces the living and the dead, the body of Adonais at last may be seen aright. When the singer returns for the third time to the grave, what he is aware of is not the "leprous corpse" but "a slope of green access/ Where, like an infant's smile, over the dead/ A light of laughing flowers along the grass is spread" (439–41). That consolation uneasily affirmed by the classical elegy—man's transformation into flower—finally is seen in the comprehensive cultural context which those elegies failed to provide. The laughing flowers are indeed Adonais because they are part of the poetic one Spirit that everywhere grows out of the earth and joyously bursts upward, imaginatively redeeming the world's body.

This perception is expanded and enriched by the poet's vision of the environment surrounding Adonais' grave, which in his narrow concentration on the "leprous corpse" he never before had really appreciated. Adonais lies in the Protestant Cemetery in Rome, becoming the avatar of the imagination's empire who has invaded and possessed the very heart of the old Roman Empire. That was an empire of the world, chained to time and secured by mortal strength and mortal weapons—enjoying the very mortal power that in section two Urania wished for poetry. But time's cycles have destroyed Rome, which becomes "at once the Paradise,/ The grave, the city, and the wilderness" (433–34). This place simultaneously reveals the imaginative truth of worldly power's inevitable failure and culture's immortality, as does the landscape of "Ozymandias." The pyramid of Caius Cestius, champion of the Roman people, stands near Adonais' grave "Like flame transformed to marble" (437), eternally bursting upward into heaven's light and so becoming the one monument of decaying Rome that has the same imaginative vitality as the new Adonais-flowers. These champions of the spirit, old and new, "waged contention with their time's decay,/ And of the past are all that cannot pass away" (431–32).

But if culture transcends the human generations, still, the individual human being does not. That was the dual perception of "Ode to the West Wind," and the poet of *Adonais* also cannot avoid seeing it. In the last five stanzas of the poem he realizes that the heavenly "burning fountain" of poetry is countered by "the fountain of [his] mourning mind" (454). Break the seal of that mortal fountain, and the tears and bitterness of section one will return. His "Heaven of Song" may have a kind of permanence insofar as it is carried on by civilization, but he himself cannot indefinitely sustain a song of such rapture. As with the orgasmic conclusion of *Epipsychidion*, the all-out commitment of the individual's energy necessarily implies its eventual exhaustion. This poet knows that he cannot forever transform death into immortality; sooner or later his poetic rapture must dwindle, leaving his "mourning mind" again to confront the world of death.

As in *Epipsychidion*, when his rapture encounters its limits he must choose the mode of its dying. Is he now to conserve himself, or to go on? In terms of the moral insights of *Adonais*, conserving himself would be a regression because it would be a return to Uranian prudence—a valuing of mere longevity over imaginative immortality. The only authentic way for this poet to go is forward, to incandescently extinguish himself, to die of happiness. In choosing to so die the singer achieves the climax of his self-development, for he transcends the self-centeredness that has trammeled his vision in the first two sections of the poem, and dies in rapture, by reaching out unendurably beyond himself toward the starry Adonais. As in *Epipsychidion*, the climax of his poem also must be its death. However, both poems have demonstrated the paradox that a generous death may be the fullest form of life.

This ending has been seen as an unforgivable destruction of the poem.[28] Indeed, it certainly is the suicide of the imagination. But the question is, could the poem end any other way? Is there really any other choice, given the assumptions of *Adonais*? Shelley shows his awareness of the question by the resemblance he suggests between the mortal waters of his poem and the waters of *Lycidas*.[29] In Shelley's poem Milton is "third among the suns of light," a poetic sun still shining although he himself "went, unterrified,/ Into the gulf of death" (35–36), that same "amorous Deep" (25) into which the starlike Adonais also has sunk. This is reminiscent of the Miltonic "remorseless deep" that swallowed Lycidas. And the conclusion of Shelley's poem is both reminiscent of, and pointedly different from, the conclusion of Milton's. Here is the final fate of Lycidas:

> Weep no more, woeful Shepherds weep no more,
> For *Lycidas* your sorrow is not dead.
> Sunk though he be beneath the wat'ry floor,
> So sinks the day-star in the Ocean bed,
> And yet anon repairs his drooping head,
> And tricks his beams, and with new-spangled Ore,
> Flames in the forehead of the morning sky:
> So *Lycidas*, sunk low, but mounted high,
> Through the dear might of him that walk'd the waves,
> Where other groves, and other streams along,
> With Nectar pure his oozy Locks he laves,
> And hears the unexpressive nuptial Song,
> In the blest Kingdoms meek of joy and love.

Like the risen Adonais, the risen Lycidas is symbolized by the morning and evening star. But Milton handles this material in a way very different from Shelley's. The Miltonic method is paradoxical: Lycidas is "sunk low, but mounted high." This sense of paradox is necessary because the resolution of the conflict, which is God's, passes beyond our understanding and can be registered there only as a mystery. God's harmonies become our miracles; "the dear might of him that walk'd the waves" restores Lycidas from the remorseless deep, although the speaker never recovers Lycidas' body or actually sees the Heaven where Lycidas' soul dwells. His poetic attempts to imagine God's world finally must be transcended through his religious faith. Therefore this rustic swain ends by rising from his poetic isolation in order to return to the normal round of life—"Tomorrow to fresh Woods and Pastures new." He can leave his moment of grief to return refreshed to his own daily business because he is sustained by the faith that God also will be going about His.

But there is no God to support the poetic vision of *Adonais*. Just as *Epipsychidion* referred to Spenser and Dante as models, *Adonais* refers to *Lycidas*; and in both cases, the Shelleyan poem creates a self-made lyrical world of the moment whereas the models exist within a Christian framework. In this perspective, the Shelleyan refusal either to hold back personal energy or to pretend that such energy can be infinite, emerges as a form of religious humility. This poet will not falsify the conditions of his being by pretending that his powers are the equivalent of God's. He has created a world of song, but that world is a transformation of life, not life itself. The poet may have godlike world-creating powers, but by accepting his own death at the poem's conclusion, he emphasizes that he is not literally God. He cannot create an eternal world; his utmost power is to create a poem that within its own terms contains everything because it implies its own beginning, development, and end. God's heaven is forever, but the poet's heaven is for the moment only; God creates reality, but the poet creates the fleeting experience of ecstasy. So poetry has both its transcendences and its limitations, and by insisting upon this, Shelley continues the feature of skeptical conclusions that figures prominently in his major poetry.

NOTES

1. Earl R. Wasserman, "Adonais," in *Shelley: A Critical Reading* (Baltimore, 1971), pp. 462–502.

2. Ibid., p. 471.

3. Ibid., p. 472.

4. Ibid., p. 487.

5. Robert Langbaum, *The Poetry of Experience: The Dramatic Monologue in Modern Literary Tradition* (New York, 1957). This poetry ". . . communicates not as truth but experience, making its circumstance ambiguously objective in order to make it emphatically someone's experience. This explains the importance of the observer or narrator or central character not only as the instrument of perception and maker of the meaning but also as the maker of the poem's validity. For there is a difference in degree of actuality between the observer and the object or circumstance, the latter being real to the extent that it is looked upon or experienced. Because the observer has the same function whether or not he bears the poet's name, we should not—in those poems where he is Wordsworth or Keats or Shelley—think of him as the man his friends knew and his biographers write about; we should rather think of him as a character in a dramatic action, a character who has been endowed by the poet with the qualities necessary to make the poem happen to him.

". . . the autobiographical illusion is . . . important as precisely the plot—a plot about the self-development of an individual . . ." (pp. 51–52).

6. Shelley probably derived this perfectibilism from the Empirical arguments of Godwin. From Book I, chapter V of *Political Justice*:

The human mind, so far as we are acquainted with it, is nothing else but a faculty of perception. All our knowledge, all our ideas, every thing we possess as intelligent beings, comes from impression. All the minds that exist, set out from absolute ignorance. They received first one impression, and then a second. As the impressions became more numerous, and were stored by the help of memory, and combined by the faculty of association, so the experience increased, and with the experience the knowledge, the wisdom, every thing that distinguishes man from what we understand by a 'clod of the valley.' This seems to be a simple and incontrovertible history of intellectual being; and, if it be true, then as our accumulations have been incessant in the time that is gone, so, as long as we continue to perceive, to remember or reflect, they must perpetually increase. Therefore, "By perfectible, it is not meant that [man] is capable of being brought to perfection. But the word seems sufficiently adapted to express the faculty of being continually made better and receiving perpetual improvement; and in this sense it is here to be understood. The term perfectible, thus explained, not only does not imply the capacity of being brought to perfection, but stands in express opposition to it. If we could arrive at perfection, there would be an end to our improvement."

7. G. Wilson Knight rather mildly observes, "What would normally be climax-impressions in poetry are here a level style." *The Starlit Dome* (London, 1959), p. 234. An amusing contemporary review, "Seraphina and Her Sister Clementina's Review of Epipsychidion" (*The Gossip*, July 14, 1821), is reprinted in Newman Ivey White, *The Unextinguished Hearth: Shelley and His Contemporary Critics* (Durham, N.C., 1938): "I read the first extract—but did not understand it. 'It is poetry *intoxicated*,' said Clementina. 'It is poetry in *delirium*,' said I. 'It is a new system of poetry,' said the gentleman, 'which may be taught by a few simple rules, and when it is learned it may be written by the leagues'" (p. 277).

8. Of course, such a position denies the idea that existence is a function of expression. See text, pp. 58–59, and 90–98 for my development of this idea. Also see Susan Hawk Brisman, "'Unsaying His High Language': The Problem of Voice in *Prometheus Unbound*," *SIR* 16, no. 1 (Winter 1977), pp. 51–86, for the development of a similar idea.

9. See text, p. 95.

10. *The Literary Criticism of William Wordsworth*, ed. Paul M. Zall (Lincoln, Nebr., 1966), p. 27.

11. For an account of Dante's and Plato's influence on *Epipsychidion*, see Neville Rogers, *Shelley at Work: A Critical Inquiry* (Oxford, 1956), pp. 230–48.

12. See text, pp. 35–36.

13. Newman Ivey White, *Shelley* (New York, 1940), II, pp. 268–69. See also Edward E. Bostetter, *The Romantic Ventriloquists: Wordsworth, Coleridge, Keats, Shelley, Byron* (Seattle, 1963): "*Epipsychidion* properly comes to an end at line 388. The part that follows is in the nature of an epilogue, almost a separate poem" (p. 198).

14. Coleridge, *The Statesman's Manual* (London, 1816), pp. 36–37.

15. As I remarked in a note to *Alastor*, Shelley's Platonizers have tended to idealize the erotic passages in his poetry. For a rebuttal, see Edward E. Bostetter, *The Romantic Ventriloquists*, p. 200: "This [passage of *Epipsychidion*] is self-evidently a description of sexual experience, of union with

a 'real' woman (as Keats would say) which is as much physical as spiritual. . . ." Also see Gerald Enscoe, "The Physical Basis of Love in Shelley's *Alastor* and *Epipsychidion*," in *Eros and the Romantics: Sexual Love as a Theme in Coleridge, Shelley and Keats* (The Hague, 1967), pp. 61–98. On p. 81 Enscoe discusses a group of Platonizing critics who have ignored the sexuality in *Epipsychidion*, the most prominent of whom are Carlos Baker and James A. Notopoulos. In *Shelley's Mythmaking* (New Haven, Conn., 1959), Harold Bloom says, "Very simply . . . "*Epipsychidion*" is a poem about heterosexual love" (p. 208). Donald H. Reiman agrees, in *Percy Bysshe Shelley* (New York, 1969): "in *Epipsychidion* the Poet, speaking in the first person, has the boldness to use sexual intercourse as a metaphor for the marriage of true minds" (p. 131). The most notable opponent of a sexual interpretation of the poem is Wasserman, who determinedly avoids noticing the eroticism in the final passage of *Epipsychidion*, describing it as follows: "What has happened is that in the very act of describing the human interpossession of himself and Emily in the world the poet exceeds the possible earthly limits until, without his intending it, the mortal context has dropped out, and he is actually describing the identity possible only in afterlife." *Shelley*, p. 460.

16. *Shelley's Prose, Or the Trumpet of a Prophecy*, ed. David Lee Clark (Albuquerque, N.M., 1954), p. 220.

17. In the most vigorous and interesting of all the attacks on *Epipsychidion*, Edward E. Bostetter argues that the relation of Shelley's poem to his life involves not only compromise, but worse, a confusion of art and life that renders the poem artistically worthless. In other words, his argument is the exact opposite of the one I make here. See "The Mutinous Flesh" in *The Romantic Ventriloquists*, pp. 198–218. In fact, the chapter of which this is a section ("Shelley," pp. 181–240) is the most cogent of all the attacks on Shelley. Bostetter founds his objections on Shelley's supposed Platonism, which he believes encouraged Shelley to aspire to an idealistic escapism from the actual world: "Withdrawal from society or the world is the end toward which most of the major poetry of Shelley moves" (p. 192). In the case of *Epipsychidion*, this escapism encourages a confusion of idealized and physical love, so that in the final erotic passage of the poem Shelley describes the act of love without really wishing to do so:

> When, at the very climax of the ecstatic union, he says that the winged words on which his soul would pierce into the height of love's rare universe are chains of lead—"I pant, I sink, I tremble, I expire!"—he means a number of things. Overtly he is referring to the futility of finding words to express the ideal relationship. . . . In addition, he realizes that he has been carried too far (for prudence) by the winged words, and so he stops abruptly and tries to avoid the obvious implications by suggesting that the words have kept him

from going far enough. . . . What follows is the inevitable aftermath of physical and mental exhaustion. But in this case there is more than exhaustion; there is frustration and defeat. He becomes aware, with the climactic words, of the futility of the dream experience; he knows that the union can never be realized . . . and he is tolled back "to his sole self." No more than with Keats can his words make the dreams come true (p. 216).

In other words, the poem has been a complex self-delusion in which the Platonizing Shelley unconsciously aims toward an actual physical experience with Emilia Viviani, and draws back in embarrassment when he senses where his "ideal" emotions are leading him. Thus, in order to maintain his Platonic sublimation, Shelley must conceive of love as follows:

. . . from human love all variety and action are to be removed; it is to be reduced to passive, trancelike faintness from which even the sex act has been eliminated or forgotten, and in which the sexual feelings are purged and purified until adults love each other as innocently as children. All conflict is eliminated from nature, and the universe dissolves into a sea of love. Human relations are reduced . . . to familial relations in a pastoral setting and a perpetual state of sentimental affection. Almost all masculine characteristics and activities have been subordinated . . .   (p. 217)

Clearly, this enervated Shelley is the very opposite of the vigorous lyrical poet that I see in *Epipsychidion*.

18. However, I do not maintain that Shelley himself is fully prepared to cope with the relentless openness of his poem, nor do I think my argument necessarily depends upon supporting such a view. I am aware that the envoi commands the poet's "Weak Verses" to

. . . call your sisters from Oblivion's cave,
All singing loud: 'Love's very pain is sweet,
But its reward is in the world divine
Which, if not here, it builds beyond the grave.'   (595–98)

Here the "sisters" of verse sing of a fictional paradise "beyond the grave," from which the harsh conditions of life are excluded. This sounds like yet another version of the third world of *Epipsychidion*—a paradise created by the transformations of poetry—but the literal suggestion that life's dissatisfactions may be ended in a perfect world beyond death cannot really be avoided in this passage.

At his best, Shelley the poet transforms the world into the form of his desires and lives abundantly, through the rhapsodic expression of his energies; at his worst, he suffers from depressions resembling those of the *Alastor* Poet, and like that Poet, he expresses a wish to die, in the hope that the paradise he cannot achieve here actually may exist "beyond the grave." Since I see his poetry as a poetry of experience rather than a poetry that probes for ontological truth, it seems to me quite possible (and in fact, the case) that in a single period of his life he can write poems that maintain both of these positions—for his poems are not truth-investigations, they are manifestations of his mood and also of his success in poetic creation.

In these terms, the lines quoted above seem to me a flaw in the poem. But it is slight, in comparison to the passages for *Epipsychidion* and the three projected prefaces that he rejected (these can be surveyed conveniently in conjunction with the poem in the Hutchinson edition). Each of these prefaces suggests that the suffering poet who wrote *Epipsychidion* is now dead, presumably killed off by the emotional ravages of his life. The materials Shelley rejected for *Epipsychidion* he did well to reject; he himself may have felt the sentimental defeatism and self-pity they express; but in excluding it from his finished poem he defended his work's organic unity and intellectual toughness. Thus, the composition of a good poem does not necessarily imply the inclusion of everything the poet actually thinks and feels; on the contrary, as in this case, it may involve a judicious exclusion.

19. Wasserman bases his entire reading of Shelley on such a distinction: the poet suffers "indecision between contradictory desires for worldly perfection and an ideal postmortal eternity" (*Shelley*, p. ix). For him, the ecstatic conclusion of *Epipsychidion* consequently demonstrates the poem's failure: "without his intending it, the mortal context has dropped out, and he is actually describing the identity possible only in afterlife. . . . A personal millennium turns out to be a future immortality" (p. 460). Wasserman then hypothesizes the composer of *Epipsychidion* standing on the pinnacle of his poem and surveying his past work in its entirety: "The whole burden of all his poems, with all their striving after the ideal, Shelley realizes as he looks back over his career, has really been that love needs a perfect world, which, if it is impossible here . . . it 'creates for itself in the infinite'" (p. 461). Thus, in spite of my great indebtedness to Wasserman's reading of *Epipsychidion*, we absolutely part company in the end. Essentially, he sees this poem as the death knell for Shelley's poetry—for the world Shelley desires cannot be created by poems, it exists only (and only possibly) beyond the grave. In contrast, I see *Epipsychidion* as a radical and spectacularly successful enactment of the poet's power to create the worlds he wishes for.

Operating within an insistently Platonic context, Ross Greig Woodman goes even farther than Wasserman in his apocalyptic readings of Shelley's later poetry. (See *The Apocalyptic Vision of the Poetry of Shelley*, University of Toronto Department of English Studies and Texts, no. 12 [Toronto, 1964].) For him, Shelley's last poems abandon the imaginative enterprise in order to pursue absolute union with the Platonic world of pure Being, an outcome predictable within a purely Platonic context (after all, Plato himself excluded the poets from his Republic). Finally, according to Woodman, "Shelley was led by Eros to annihilate the world of his imaginative vision, to reject his earlier Promethean role as 'the savior and strength of suffering man.' . . . Shelley was . . . forced in the end to realize that the roles of Eros and the imagination are incompatible. The way of the imagination is the way of incarnation, . . . the way of Eros is the way of transcendence. In terms of Eros, the incarnation is but a dim vapour that veils the omnipotent spirit" (p. 197).

Bloom posits a version of apocalypse that, on the whole, seems to me rather more adequate. From *The Ringers in the Tower: Studies in Romantic Tradition* (Chicago and London, 1971):

> Lyrical poetry at its most intense frequently moves toward direct address between one human consciousness and another, in which the "I" of the poet directly invokes the personal "Thou" of the reader. . . . Shelley converts forms as diverse as drama, prose essay, romance, satire, epyllion, into lyric. To an extent he himself scarcely realized, Shelley's genius desired a transformation of all experience, natural and literary, into the condition of lyric. More than all other poets, Shelley's compulsion is to present life as a direct confrontation of equal realities. This compulsion seeks absolute intensity, and courts straining and breaking in consequence. When expressed as love, it must manifest itself as mutual destruction. . . . Shelley is the poet of these flames, and he is equally the poet of a particular shadow, which falls perpetually between all such flames, a shadow of ruin that tracks every imaginative flight of fire. . . . By the time Shelley had reached his final phase . . . he had become altogether the poet of this shadow of ruin, and had ceased to celebrate the possibilities of imaginative relationship" (pp. 88–89).

I agree with all of this, except for the final sentence. Bloom's apocalypse of experience, it seems, implies destruction as much as does Wasserman's and Woodman's apocalypse of transcendence. In place of the notion of destruction I would suggest the notion of exhaustion, with a biological grounding. In this perspective, what we see in Shelley's later poetry is not a failure of imagination but the lyrical exhaustion of physical energies. The tension, then, is not between apocalypse and millennium but between the infinite imaginative scope of spirit and the limited resources of the human body, as it also is in the work of Byron and Schopenhauer.

20. Of course, these remarks retrospectively apply to "Ode to the West Wind." There the poet triumphs over a merely natural death by extinguishing himself in the generous raptures of his own lyricism.

21. The translation of Bion and Moschus used in this chapter is from

The Greek Bucolic Poets, ed. and trans. A. S. F. Gow (Cambridge, Mass., 1953).

22. "This term Splendour for any immaterial substance is borrowed from Dante: 'Vid'io così più turbe de *Splendori* fulguranti [folgoranti, Temple ed.] in su.' Parad. xxiii [82–83] 'The Splendour that had lit on the lips of.'" Richard Harter Fogle, "John Taafe's Annotated Copy of Adonais," *KSJ* 17 (1968), 31–52.

23. See Wasserman's analysis of the fire/water symbolic complex in *Adonais*. *Shelley*, pp. 466–502.

24. The most powerful statement of this position is by Edward E. Bostetter, in *The Romantic Ventriloquists*:

The physical and psychological reaction that Shelley associated with love was enervation. In fact, it was his reaction to every major emotional and sensuous experience. It was, whatever its ultimate cause, perhaps the basic pattern of his nature. His most consistently held conception of himself is of the strong man drained of strength. He contemplates this portrait with pity, and yet with pride . . . sometimes he sees the loss of power as a sign of his sensitivity, as the price he must pay for having gazed on "Nature's naked loveliness," as the inevitable result of the pursuit of the ideal. It becomes the mark of his superiority to other men. The self-portrait in *Adonais* is the most striking illustration of this attitude" (pp. 213–14).

Other critics who condemn the self-portrait in *Adonais* include Desmond King-Hele, *Shelley: His Thought and Work* (London, 1960), p. 307; Graham Hough, *The Romantic Poets* (London, 1953), p. 146; Carl Grabo, *The Magic Plant: The Growth of Shelley's Thought* (Chapel Hill, N.C., 1936), pp. 365–66; and Milton Wilson, *Shelley's Later Poetry: A Study of His Prophetic Imagination* (New York, 1959), pp. 2 and 5. For a defense of Shelley's self-portraits, see Judith Chernaik, "The Figure of the Poet," in *The Lyrics of Shelley* (Cleveland and London, 1972), pp. 8–31. In particular, I am in sympathy with Chernaik's view that Shelley's self-portraits are concerned with the conflict between spiritual aspirations and physical limitations: "As he enters into the limitless aspiration of the spirit, so he recognizes and laments the frailty of the body to which the spirit is bound" (pp. 29–30).

25. Wasserman's view that Shelley's poems are explorations in search of ontological truth undergoes a radical conversion on p. 472 of *Shelley*: "The skeptic's first principle is not an axiom or a dogma but only some unassertive and disordered objects of perception; their meaning is a function of the form into which the poet's mind draws them, and his successive tentative faiths are not convictions but only aesthetic decisions. The credible "truth" the poem [*Adonais*] finally achieves is born entirely out of the errors and half-truths of aesthetic inadequacies." Apparently,

for Wasserman's Shelley, Truth finally becomes Beauty—in itself, a statement no less inadequate to account for Shelley than to account for Keats. Wasserman's final truth-standard seems to be a thoroughgoing aestheticism. But as my analysis of *Adonais* tries to demonstrate, the aesthetic transformations of the poem are grounded in moral transformations. This poem is not an impersonal search for Beauty—it is the beautiful drama of a person's moral development.

26. As Bloom says in *The Ringers in the Tower*: "Though *Adonais* has been extensively Platonized and Neoplatonized by a troop of interpreters, it is in a clear sense a materialist's poem, written out of a materialist's despair at his own deepest convictions, and finally a poem soaring above those convictions into a mystery that leaves a pragmatic materialism quite undisturbed" (p. 111).

See also John Wright's reading in *Shelley's Myth of Metaphor* (Athens, Ga., 1970, pp. 59–73), which argues against the "supernaturalist literalism" with which Wasserman treats the poem (p. 60). Wright suggests that *Adonais* and *A Defence of Poetry* "illuminate and illustrate each other," because both feature "the vision of the mind as a field filled with evidences in the transfiguration of metaphor into myth of the unity and communion of the human spirit" (p. 73).

27. Note the image of the fire-fountain in the passage quoted from the *Essay on Christianity* (p. 139).

28. As usual, the most powerful condemnation comes from Bostetter, in *The Romantic Ventriloquists*: "There is no pretense here of perfectibility; the only escape from the nightmare of life is death. A distinction is drawn between the hideous dream of human life and the beauty of the physical universe, which is the outward manifestation and expression of the ideal with which Adonais becomes one at his death. At the end, therefore, the poem becomes an hypnotic exhortation to self-destruction" (p. 224). See also Milton Wilson's "From Heaven or Near It" in *Shelley's Later Poetry*, pp. 236–55. Wilson stacks the deck by first proclaiming what funeral elegies ought to do: "Even on the earthly level there are ways in which a man's death is not the end of him, and the elegy can test such compensations. . . . Of these the most commonly invoked are survival in memory, survival in creations (institutions, works of art, children), and material survival in nature. The first two are often combined, and (excluding children) we may put them both under the broad heading of fame, a subject about which elegies have traditionally had a good deal to say" (p. 242). Since Wilson sees Shelley driving singlemindedly toward a personal Platonic apocalypse in *Adonais*, he finds the poem's conclusion to be lacking the social sensibility that he considers essential in the elegy: "At the end of *Adonais* we can imagine the mourn-

ers, headed by Shelley, waiting in single file for their own private apocalypses, but we do not see anything like the giant Albion awakening in Blake's Jerusalem" (p. 255).

29. For a discussion of Milton and Miltonic echoes in *Adonais*, see Frederick L. Jones, "Shelley and Milton," *SP* 49, no. 3 (July 1952), pp. 488–519.

CHAPTER SIX

Transforming Hell: *The Triumph of Life*

It was Shelley's death, and not his own poetic finality, that brought an end to *The Triumph of Life*. Had he lived, his poem might have grown much longer, or it might have ended a few lines beyond where it now does. Anyone who attempts a reading of the poem at least implicitly must decide whether it is a virtual whole or a part, for different procedures will govern the interpretation of a finished work as opposed to a fragment.

I believe *The Triumph of Life* indeed is a fragment, and my opinion is based on the formal resemblance of this poem to two of Shelley's earlier, completed works—*Epipsychidion* and *Adonais*.[1] *The Triumph of Life* was written in spring and early summer of 1822, following reasonably closely upon *Epipsychidion* (January and February 1821) and *Adonais* (June 1821), and there seems to be a consistent line of development running through these poems. All three are told from the viewpoint of a singer who participates in the poem's action, and, at least in *Epipsychidion* and *Adonais*, successive changes in this singer's outlook transform his world. I have called *Epipsychidion* and *Adonais* dramatic lyrics because they show transformation being created by song. In them world-view is manifested as a singer's essential self—a lyric outpouring—and it follows that if the singer is poet enough to make a new song, he will inherit a new world. *Epipsychidion* and *Adonais* both begin in fallen lyric worlds decreed and yet not desired by their singers. The poems then move through a series of transformations in pursuit of the singer's desire, until it is successfully embodied in its own proper heaven.

Clearly, Shelley's models for *The Triumph of Life* potentially suggest similar transformations. Petrarch's *Triumphs*, which supplies the poem's title and its chariot of Life, is a dialectical series of six poetic triumphal processions, each of which conquers its predecessor, until the progress culminates in *The Triumph of Eternity*. More important, there is *The Divine Comedy*, with its progress from hell, to purgatory, and finally to heaven.[2] Shelley's Rousseau, who as the guide to his triumph is equivalent to Dante's Vergil, describes Dante's poem in terms that would better fit a Shelleyan dramatic lyric:

> "Behold a wonder worthy of the rhyme
>
> "Of him whom from the lowest depths of Hell
> Through every Paradise & through all glory
> Love led serene, & who returned to tell
>
> "In words of hate & awe the wondrous story
> How all things are transfigured, except Love;[3]

This Dante sees Love as the first principle of the world and does not even mention God—an omission inconceivable for Dante himself. Everywhere Shelley's poet has wandered he has seen Love as the only constant in a universe of incessant transformation. That equally well could be asserted of the worlds of

Epipsychidion and *Adonais*, which come into existence because of love for Emily and Adonais and then are transformed repeatedly because a context, a proper place for that love, must be created. When it takes form, the Shelleyan heaven is purely an organization of the appearances that allows for love. But Dante's and Petrarch's Paradise is a real place created by God, which means that no matter how much change they see in the world, they will believe that behind appearance is a divine unchanging reality. The poems written out of such notions become versions of the pilgrimage, in which Dante and Petrarch undertake spiritual journeys to come nearer to God. Shelley assumes that heaven is within the eye of the beholder; consequently, his paradise ought to lie in a transformation of the appearances. In other words, the paradise of *The Triumph of Life* ought not to be elsewhere and otherwise, but simply to be the same place and circumstances seen differently. So what I will be looking for in the *Triumph* could be termed "transformability"—indications that the poem's hellish appearances invite heavenly transformations. If this seems to be the case, we could infer that the existing *Triumph* is the first section of a dramatic lyric which if completed might have formally resembled *Epipsychidion* and *Adonais*.

To begin, one must recall what comprises heaven in the worlds of Shelley's dramatic lyrics. In *Epipsychidion* heaven is a perfectly expressive sexuality, and in *Adonais* it is a deathless rapture felt at the very brink of the grave. Both experiences are variations of what could be called the infinite moment.[4] By their very nature, they can last only briefly, but if they are completely surrendered to they elicit the ideal perfection of human powers. To say that such moments pass is less important than to affirm that they exist; indeed, their very fragility and rarity is in itself a powerful argument for their great value. What the final movements of *Epipsychidion* and *Adonais* render is an expression of this heavenly infinite moment. Through the dramatic experience of the poem's lyricist, the reader himself sees what it would be like to achieve the apotheosis of the imagination.

In pointed contrast, *The Triumph of Life* shows the human world as a triumphal procession of slaves compelled to surround Life's chariot by various individual compulsions. The victims find themselves in this hell because they thirst for an experience of infinity—their own proper infinity, which would be complete satisfaction of their particular desires. Each person sees this infinity not as a special way of existing in the present but as the insatiable challenge of an unpossessed desire which maddeningly refuses to be subjected to his will. Everyone lusts to have more or to do more, and they all go about it by speeding up their life processes—by forcibly trying to pack as much experience as possible into each moment. Clearly, these are the methods of hell, not of heaven; for the captives' rage to live only succeeds in exhausting their physical and spiritual resources with unnatural swiftness. Life dominates them because they discover that the pursuit of their desires inevitably must be paid for by the sacrifice of their lives. It is their very longing for heaven that delivers them into hell.

The human space and time created by this maddening urge to live is in itself a rhythm, a dance, a poem; the poetic narrator has the eye to bring out this aspect of the triumphal procession. He sees that the slaves throw themselves into a "wild dance" in which they "Mix with each other in tempestuous measure/ To savage music" that is their own "agonizing pleasure" (141–43), killing themselves with what they love. Just as this dance accelerates human time, it also deforms human space: the world of hell becomes a vague matrix of rapidly shifting appearances. Shadows, clouds, and phantoms surround the triumphal procession—and nothing seen there is to be trusted because it will not last long. As Rousseau says, the world is like a bubble, and upon it, "Figures ever new/ Rise . . . We have but thrown, as those before us threw,/ Our shadows on it as it past away" (248–51).

If the law of Shelley's heaven is imaginative transformation, the transfiguration of worlds that occurs through the perception of transforming images, then in this triumphal procession we see the corresponding Shelleyan hell. Here there is no stillness, no imagery that lasts long enough to become the unmoving center that could change the world. Transformation becomes a curse instead of a blessing because *everything* moves perpetually and with a swiftness that makes any kind of orientation impossible. In this world the heaven of transformation becomes the hell of illusion, and the inevitable fate of human beings caught in this dance of shadows is to suffer physical and spiritual deformity. So, "From every firmest limb & fairest face/ The strength & freshness fell like dust" (520–21), and worse yet, people melt away into "phantoms, & the air/ Was peopled with dim forms" (482–83), or become "elves" who "Danced in a thousand unimagined shapes" (490–91) or "restless apes" (493), "vultures" (497), or even "small gnats & flies" (508).

Not only are individuals deformed and driven to a premature death in this triumph; the very history of Western civilization demonstrates the same pathology. Rousseau says he has seen "The progress of the pageant since the morn," and that the narrator may be curious enough to "Follow it thou even to the night, but I/ Am weary" (193–95). Apparently, then, this procession lasts only for a day; yet that day is not only the entire lifetime of Rousseau and presumably the poem's narrator but also the whole life of Europe. Men become gnats that live only a summer's day, and history becomes a vanishing apparition painted upon the world's bubble. In contrast to Dante's Inferno, which is eternal, this Shelleyan pageant is hell because it lasts practically no time at all.

This explains the speaker's need for orientation. In a perpetually transforming world, how can you know where you are? Rousseau, whom he mistakenly has perceived as "an old root which grew/ To strange distortion out of the hill side," with "holes it vainly sought to hide" which "Were or had been eyes" (182–88), arises unnervingly, a distortion in a distorted landscape, to become his guide. As Dante was guided through the Inferno by a fellow poet, so is this narrator. But while Vergil is a true poet, a reliable interpreter of appearances, the judgments of Shelley's deformed and possibly blinded Rousseau must be regarded with skepticism. In fact, this Rousseau turns out to be the proper poet of hell, a singer who creates hell's very rhythms—the tempos that burn through the blood, that cause listeners to throw themselves into the wild dance of self-destruction. Rousseau "feared, loved, hated, suffered, did, & died" (200), and transformed his maelstrom of passions into poetry, a form that can infect others. Indeed, he speaks of ancient poetry as a "contagion" that "infected" its audience (277–78), and he adds, "I/ Am one of those who have created, even/ If it be but a world of agony" (293–95).[5]

This remark recalls Shelley's Prometheus, who through his lyric curse created a world of agony, and also Beatrice Cenci, who mourns "what a world we make,/ The oppressor and the oppressed." Like Beatrice's world, Rousseau's is a world of the oppressor and the oppressed; like Prometheus, he contains these universal relations within himself. As he says, "I was overcome/ By my own heart alone" (240–41). Apparently, the triumph of Life has power to dominate Rousseau only because it images his own process of self-subjection. The poet of hell is divided against himself; he advises the narrator that the only choice is "from spectator" to "turn/ Actor or victim in this wretchedness" (305–6). Actor or victim, oppressor or oppressed—in Rousseau's world as in Prometheus' and Beatrice's, one is forced to play the part of either tyrant or slave.

In *The Triumph of Life* this vision of the world seems to explain modern European history. The greatest modern conqueror, Napoleon, becomes a political version of Rousseau, a creature of insatiable desires who "sought to win/ The world, and lost all that it did contain/ Of greatness, in its hope destroyed" (217–19). Rousseau and Napoleon exemplify those Promethean revolutionary hopes that end in destruction because those who avow them are not whole men. Like the kings of thought enslaved in the triumph,

> "their lore
>
> "Taught them not this—to know themselves;
>   their might
> Could not repress the mutiny within,
>   And for the morn of truth they feigned, deep night
>
> "Caught them ere evening."
>
>   (211–15)

It seems that an experience of self-analysis and growth is necessary to transform the vision of Life seen in the *Triumph*. The real problem is not whether to "turn/ Actor or victim" in the pageant, but how to convert the global tyrant/slave view of relationship into another offering different options.[6]

In fact, two world views are suggested in the existing *Triumph*—the way of Life, which seems to dominate Rousseau's perceptions and for the time being also the narrator's, and the way of the visionary "shape all light" (352) beheld by Rousseau in his youth. These figures show telling resemblances but at the same time are substantially different; for Life is a foil to the shape all light. If the shape all light is a woman, it is less obvious but nevertheless clear that Life also is female: Rousseau refers to this figure three times as "her" (438, 441, 443), and unwittingly, the speaker describes her in terms parodying the shape all light—she is the "Shape . . . whom years deform" (87–88). He also compares her to the "dead Mother" of the new moon being borne in its arms (84), and the tempestuous motion and cloudy shifting of shapes in Life's triumph certainly justifies this image. In contrast, Rousseau has seen the shape all light as divinely still, miraculously walking upon a stream at her own pace, rather than being borne away by the natural flow of the water. Her movement is a rhythm, a poem, a world of "wondrous music," "the ceaseless song/ Of leaves & winds & waves & birds & bees/ And falling drops" which "moved in a measure new/ Yet sweet" (369, 375–78). She is a counterforce to Life, a possibility of quietness that, like the still vision of the mountain peak in "Mont Blanc," might open the way to orientation in a world plagued by excessive, dizzying movement. She so slows time by her joyful poetry that it is practically arrested: her Eden is a stately rapture, a version of the infinite moment. She is a transforming image, and the man who learns her rhythms could be the poet of heaven.

And yet, Rousseau's experience with her is destructive, just as is the *Alastor* Poet's vision of his ideal lady. But in both cases, it is not necessarily the vision itself that is to blame—it could be the way in which that vision is interpreted by its beholder. There are indications of this in the way Rousseau retells his experience. Indeed, the very fact that in the *Triumph* we hear his version of events rather than witnessing them ourselves should be a clear signal that this tale is an interpretation of experience rather than experience itself. Thus, the very narrative form of the poem requires us to examine critically what Rousseau says.[7]

He starts by saying that one morning he awakened as though born again, in a strange new landscape and without memory of his prior life. The world he confronts is a paradise, a dawning Eden that opens its promise to him. Yet he cannot feel completely at ease within it. Faintly but persistently he remains disturbed that he cannot remember his past—even though he realizes it very well may be better forgotten. He cannot quite believe in the present, either. He refers to his surroundings as "this valley of perpetual dream," a distrustful suggestion significantly amplified by his question to the shape all light: "Show whence I came, and where I am, and why—/ Pass not away upon the passing stream" (397–99). Apparently Rousseau cannot feel that the edenic here and now is the only reality that matters. What he wants to know is the shape of the past, and what he fears is the shape of the future—that his vision may pass away "upon the passing stream," even though he can see that far from flowing away with the stream, the shape all light miraculously walks upon the waters. His is a time-ridden sensibility, not one that can find eternity in the present. In order to feel oriented, he must control knowledge of all his time, which he senses as a world extending far into the past and vanishing far into the future. So when the shape all light commands him to "Arise and quench thy thirst" (400), he receives the kind of temporal world he thirsts for—but to his sorrow discovers that in such a world thirst is limitless and therefore unquenchable. Like the oracular statements of Demogorgon, which must be interpreted by Asia in order to mean anything, the shape all light's cryptic command is given content by the essential being of the person who obeys it.

A passage from one of Shelley's last letters echoes Rousseau's situation. To John Gisborne on 18 June 1822 he writes, "I have a boat here . . it is swift and beautiful, and appears quite a vessel. Williams is captain, and we drive along this delightful bay in the evening wind, under the summer moon, until earth appears another world. Jane brings her guitar, and if the past and the future could be obliterated, the present would content me so well that I could say with Faust to the passing moment, 'Remain, thou, thou art so beautiful.'"[8] The ideal Faustian desire that the present moment remain, felt while driving along in one's boat under the summer moon, is "another world" valid at the moment but soon fated to be replaced by awareness of "the past and the future."[9]

Shelley's heaven is not forever but for the moment, which is what we would expect in a world of moving appearances, of transformations. Just as Shelley's boat races along in the wind, so heaven itself must be involved in movement. The heaven of sexual climax in *Epipsychidion* can last only a moment, and the imaginative transfiguration into eternal life in *Adonais* is built upon the brink of the grave.

In fact, by the end of his career Shelley entirely has transformed the desire that initiated it. We have seen the young idealist of *On Life*, who wrote *Alastor*, proclaiming that "man is a being of high aspirations . . . existing but in the future and the past; being, not what he is, but what he has been and shall be." [10] But in Shelley's letter to John Gisborne, that desire to dwell in the future and the past has become a recognition that "the present would content me so well" if only it could be entered into completely. The mature Shelley sees heaven as *now*—and the difficulty of reaching heaven becomes precisely the difficulty of giving up the future and the past, of surrendering oneself so totally to the lyrical present that time is annihilated. [11] Both Shelley and his creation, Rousseau, sense the challenge and the threat of this self-abandonment: not only does it bring one into heaven, it also brings one swiftly to death—for the true lyricist necessarily must commit all his energies, must sing himself to exhaustion.

If the poet holds back, refuses to embrace the perfect moment, the result will be an immediate return to the world of "the future and the past"—death by the triumph of Life. So the Shelleyan poet faces an inescapable dilemma: no matter which way he turns, he will encounter some form of death. But there is a choice to be made, after all; it involves a matter of values. The death of Life is the death of selfishness, the impossible but irresistible drive to appropriate infinity *for* oneself; the death of heaven is the death of generosity, the total surrender of one's selfhood *to* the world in pursuit of relationship, of more than self-conditioned value. The expired lyricists of *Epipsychidion* and *Adonais* leave behind their poems, as gifts bestowed upon civilization, and they see a form of salvation in selflessness and civility. In contrast, the expired Rousseau and Napoleon of *The Triumph of Life* leave behind their words and deeds as "a world of agony," and so naturally they see history as the triumph of Life—but we can see that they themselves have contributed to that triumph. Where the true Shelleyan poet fabricates civilization, they fashion a barbaric parody of it.

The evolution of Rousseau and Napoleon is not a function of historical necessity, as Rousseau's vision of the triumph of Life seems to imply. Rousseau needs to see that he has made his own world—that, contrary to his own belief, he has the power of choice. A typical Shelleyan literalist, he believes that his images are the only possible images and that they can mean only one thing. *The Triumph of Life* vividly illustrates the hopelessness, the feeling of powerlessness, created by such an attitude. Rousseau is the disillusioned *Alastor* Poet deepened and writ large, the poet who can be dangerous to himself and to mankind because he does not understand his own processes of creativity.

That the existing world of the *Triumph* need not be so is suggested by Rousseau's own words, although doubtless he is not aware of their implication. He says that the shape all light was overborne by the louder music and more vivid light of Life, but still her "obscure tenour keep[s]/ Beside my path, as silent as a ghost" (432–33). There she awaits Rousseau and the narrator, her world a latent poetic context of appearances. If their perceptions changed, this world could coalesce and emerge into the foreground, as similar heavenly worlds in fact do in *Epipsychidion* and *Adonais*.[12] But no matter what world they choose to see, all is poetry, all is commitment, all is motion. Be it the disintegrations and discords of hell or the rhythms and melodies of heaven, their world—their space and their time—is their own creation. In

Shelley's vision this becomes not a self-congratulatory situation but a constant challenge to create and sustain being. We continually must sing out our world and continually must choose what it is to become.

NOTES

1. In his latest reading of Shelley, Harold Bloom argues that *The Triumph of Life* is both complete and a fragment—or, really, that the distinction I attempt to draw between a completed poem and a fragment is irrelevant. See *Poetry and Repression: Revisionism from Blake to Stevens* (New Haven and London, 1976), p. 99:

> . . . there are, of course, no "unfinished" strong poems; there are only stronger and weaker poems. The idea of a "finished" poem itself depends upon the absurd, hidden notion that reifies poems from relationships into entities. As a poem is not even so much a relationship between entities, as it is a relationship between relationships, or a Peircean Idea of Thirdness, we can say that no relationship between relationships can ever be finished *or* unfinished except quite arbitrarily. A monad presumably can be finished; perhaps a dyad can be left unfinished; but a modern poem is a triad, which is why it begins in a dialectical alternation of presence and absence, and why it ends in a transumptive interplay of earliness and lateness. . . .

We can map the *Triumph* therefore as the complete poem it is, while remembering that a phrase like "complete poem" is oxymoronic.

2. For the influence of Dante and Petrarch on *The Triumph of Life*, see Donald H. Reiman, "A Reading of 'The Triumph of Life,' " in *Shelley's "The Triumph of Life": A Critical Study, Based on a Text Newly Edited from the Bodleian Manuscript* (Urbana, Ill. 1965), pp. 19–86. Reiman also sees *Comus* as an influence on Shelley's poem.

3. The text of *The Triumph of Life* referred to in this chapter is from Reiman, *Shelley's "The Triumph of Life."*

4. For a brief discussion of this moment, see "Moments," in M. H. Abrams, *Natural Supernaturalism: Tradition and Revolution in Romantic Literature* (New York, 1971), pp. 385–90.

5. For the influence of Rousseau on *The Triumph of Life*, see Reiman, *Shelley's "The Triumph of Life,"* pp. 58–85. Reiman very astutely emphasizes the relevance of Rousseau's *Julie, ou la Nouvelle Heloise*, to Shelley's concerns. This novel was one of Shelley's favorites. The relationship of Julie and St. Preux is a story of Romantic unattainable love and has interesting relations to the hopeless, idealistic love of the *Alastor* Poet and Shelley's other unfulfilled lovers.

6. For an account of the tyrant/slave relationship in *Prometheus Unbound*, see pp. 71–77.

7. The significance of the "shape all light" has been a focus for the critical analysis of *The Triumph of Life*. Some interpreters, such as Baker, Cameron, and King-Hele, see the "shape" as a beneficent force; others, such as Bloom and Bostetter, see her as malevolent. I see her as a cryptic transforming image, rendered meaningful by what Rousseau himself makes of her. In this perspective, I believe many critics of the *Triumph* themselves fall into Rousseau's role, making the "shape all light" reflect their attitudes toward the poem as a whole. Here is a selection of interpretations of the "shape," which will illustrate the amazing diversity of opinion. Harold Bloom: "Rousseau is betrayed to the light of Life because he began by yielding his imagination's light to the lesser but seductive light of nature, represented in the poem by the 'Shape all light' who offers him the waters of natural experience to drink" (*The Ringers in the Tower: Studies in Romantic Tradition* [Chicago and London, 1971], p. 114). Edward E. Bostetter: "The whole of Rousseau's experience is a dream, and of the nature of ultimate reality he has no evidence beyond his dream. Could it be that the vision of life is the ultimate reality, and the dream of the ideal the illusion?" (*The Romantic Ventriloquists: Wordsworth, Coleridge, Keats, Shelley, Byron* [Seattle, 1963], pp. 188–89). Carlos Baker: "Shelley reincarnated in woman's shape his conception of the source of true poetic power—this time as Iris, many-colored goddess of the rainbow, prismatic reflector of the rays of the supernal sun" (*Shelley's Major Poetry: The Fabric of a Vision* [New York, 1948, 1961], pp. 264–65). Desmond King-Hele: "[the "shape all light"] might be described as the essence of what is seen or felt by those who think they have had mystic communion with some higher power, but it may also be intended to represent merely the guiding light of those who have high ideals" (*Shelley: His Thought and Work* [London, 1960], p. 353). Kenneth Cameron: ". . . she is a manifestation of nature, and she comes 'from the realm without a name,' that is, from the unknown essence of the universe" (*Shelley: The Golden Years* [Cambridge, Mass., 1974], pp. 463–64).

8. *The Letters of Percy Bysshe Shelley*, ed. Frederick L. Jones, 2 vols. (Oxford, 1964), II, pp. 435–36.

9. Neville Rogers prints this poem, "scribbled in pencil on a page of the manuscript" of the *Triumph*:

> The hours are flying
> And joys are dying
> And hope is sighing
>   There is
> Far more to fear

> In the coming year
> Than desire can bear
> In this

Neville Rogers, *Shelley at Work: A Critical Inquiry* (Oxford, 1956), p. 288.

10. See text, p. 25.

11. Donald Reiman also refers to Shelley's letter to John Gisborne, but draws conclusions about it, and about the *Triumph*, that are the opposite of mine: "'The Triumph of Life' reflects . . . Shelley's continuing refusal to immerse himself completely in the pleasures of the moment. . . . if men were angels, if the laws of cause and effect were suspended, if moral considerations and the woes of the entire suffering earth were of no concern to Shelley—then he could wish the present moment of innocent pleasure an eternity. But the still, sad music of humanity reverberating in his soul would not let him completely temper himself to the season, subdue himself to the element that surrounded him, and contribute to the evils that he lamented by his hypocrisy." *Shelley's "The Triumph of Life,"* p. 86.

12. Reiman and Bloom, the two most distinguished critics of this poem, come to opposite conclusions. Bloom says, "By the time Shelley had reached his final phase . . . he had become altogether the poet of . . . ruin, and had ceased to celebrate the possibilities of imaginative relationship" (*The Ringers in the Tower*, p. 89). See also "The Triumph of Life" in *Shelley's Mythmaking* (New Haven, Conn., 1959, pp. 220–75), and especially p. 249, where Bloom discusses the collapse of Shelley's myth of relationship.

In contrast, Reiman sees a qualified optimism in the poem. For him the "shape all light" "proves to be a vision of the Ideal as it is distorted both by the limitations of the human condition and by those of the individual mind" (*Percy Bysshe Shelley* [New York, 1969], p. 157). In believing in her wholly, Rousseau is "absolutizing the relative and . . . seeking within the limited world of mutability the vision of what was eternal and unconditional"; and thereby he "has blinded himself to the virtue and beauty of sublunar things without having found anything with which to replace them" (pp. 157–58). Consequently, "The problem for Shelley, as for all idealists, was to maintain his vision of the Ideal while living effectively within the limitations of the sublunary, actual world" (*Shelley's "The Triumph of Life,"* p. 85).

I see neither the ruin of all hope envisioned by Bloom, nor the transcendental idealism argued for by Reiman (especially in *Shelley's "The Triumph of Life"*). It seems to me that the stress of the poem is on transformation: the world of the *Triumph* is what its poet will make of it.

The Enterprise of Transformation

Having finished a reading of Shelley's major poems, we now can make a few final observations about his development as a poet and the kind of poetry he writes.

Alastor is the first work clearly to formulate the Shelleyan sense of being in the world. It says, *I dream of my beloved, and move through the world in a hopeless search for her until I die.* The later work avoids this disillusioned death by transforming the world into the shape of the poet's desires. Shelley's mature poetry says, *I see a vision and pursue it through a transforming world until finally I embrace my dream—which has become a version of myself.* By his activity the poet changes the world into an image of his ideal self; or to put it another way, he writes a poem. But at the crowning moment of his achievement he must encounter the effects of his own effort: *It is finished.* Paradoxically, his very success implies its own proper failure, for the minute he grasps what he is moving toward, all movement ceases in the finality of fulfillment.

Shelley's poetry of transformation can transcend the ending of individual poems only by moving on to the creation of new ones. His method, which calls for incessant transformations within poems themselves, also calls for the incessant creation of new poetry. This poetry is a version of the poetry of transcendence because in its constant movement it opts for not here but there, not the object but its potential, not the real but the ideal. However, it emphatically is not transcendentalist. Unlike transcendental poetry, which says, *I look through the object to see a higher reality*, Shelleyan poetry simply says, *The object transforms, and this lures me onward*. Transcendentalism goes *through*; Shelley goes *farther*—and must keep going indefinitely, for there is no transcendental finality for him to rest in, only objects that beckon from ahead, inviting new transformations. His world is a world of relentless openness, in which truths constantly are being formulated but no final vision of Truth is possible. Since his world is actually a transformed version of himself, another way of describing this openness is to say that his poems incessantly formulate new versions of himself but never can unveil an underlying Real Self. Shelley's poetry relates self and world through the act of transformation: he is what he makes, so to continue existing he constantly must be making things anew.

It is not surprising that in the earlier years of this century there was a revolt against Shelley. Leavis complained that he could not rest in the object ("there is nothing grasped in the poetry—no object offered for contemplation, no realized presence to persuade or move us by what it is. . . . Shelley, at his best and worst, offers the emotion in itself, unattached, in the void").[1] Eliot objected to his idealism, which seemed facile ("an enthusiasm for Shelley seems to me . . . to be an affair of adolescence. . . . I was intoxicated by Shelley's poetry at the age of fifteen, and now find it almost unreadable").[2] Both protests are forms of Arnold's even more famous observation that Shelley "is a beautiful and *ineffec-*

tual angel, beating in the void his luminous wings in vain."[3] By now, an increasing appreciation of Shelley's artistic method has helped counter Leavis's technical objections. We can see it is parochial to demand that all poetry must seek some kind of rest in the object, even if this is the mode that now prevails—for this unnecessarily limits the possible varieties of poetry.[4] However, an objection to Shelley's high-flying idealism still seems possible: one can say, I see that he does what he does well, but I am not touched by it.

I hope that my emphasis upon Shelley's skepticism would help moderate the view of those who feel this way. He inherits a philosophical skepticism from the British Empiricists, founded upon the Empirical inability to perceive a necessary ontological connection between any cause and effect, any one perception and the next. In his hands this becomes a poetic skepticism. He sees transforming images entering the lacunae between one perception and the next; and if these are holy, a manifestation of the divinity within us, still, every individual possibly harbors a different divinity. Mont Blanc can be the image of imaginative love or of Ahriman because what we see in our moments of vision is not transcendental truth but the transformed image of ourselves. This transformed image is doubly indirect because in itself it does not intrinsically display meaning—it simply is a cryptic appearance which we ourselves must construe. The transforming vision is not the visitation of a mysterious authority from within; it is an invitation to movement, an evocative image that draws us out into interpretation. And the poet knows that such images can sustain an indefinitely large number of readings. Hence, an adequate idealism must be sophisticated rather than naive, poetic rather than literal, transformational rather than ontological. Religion is transformed into poetry when we realize that our gods are made by ourselves. Since we make them in our own image, we also must allow others the freedom to make their own gods in their own way. A poem by Shelley typically ends by calling itself into question—either by an actual question, as in "Mont Blanc" and "Ode to the West Wind," or by a fearless self-destruction, as in *Epipsychidion* and *Adonais*, which calls attention to the poem not as a real world but as a poetic world, not as truth but as a vision.

Himself a notorious enthusiast, as a poet Shelley has worked out an interesting accommodation between idealistic enthusiasm and skepticism. As he grew older, his Empirical skepticism, and presumably, his experience of life, made him increasingly dubious about making sweeping assertions and plans of action. But as the Preface to *Prometheus Unbound* argues, moral action becomes impossible without the ability to "love, and admire, and trust, and hope, and endure." The Shelleyan poem becomes a world in which the expression of enthusiasm is possible because it is a cosmos in which cause and effect are shaped and connected by its maker into a vision of his hopes. Unlike the actual world, where we forever must remain skeptical about such connections, the poem is globally controllable. Within its confines, the poet can demonstrate his absolute freedom and power—which for the later Shelley means that he can work toward a formulation that releases completely rapturous self-expression. Forsaking the pursuit of ontology, he commits himself to the pursuit of experience. And in his hands the lyric becomes a form that by creating experience, creates a self. Expression and existence become dual aspects of a unity; within these terms, a good poem becomes one that builds a world in which experience can be ideally maximized. If the emotional growth experienced in such poetry is not the same as the emotional growth experienced in life, nevertheless, the sophisticated idealist can make connections between the two. Poetry is a world of perfect feeling which may help its sensitive readers to cultivate a feeling for life. If Shelley is an idealist, we must emphasize that he is an empirically oriented idealist whose poetry calls for a skeptical application of idealism to life.

Another way of describing this indirect relation of the Shelleyan poem to life is to observe that for Shelley, poetry becomes a humanist version of paradise. The eternity and perfection available for Christians in heaven are transferred by this atheistic poet to the world of poetry. The result is his very great emphasis upon culture, both in A Defence of Poetry and in the poems studied in this volume. On the one hand his vision of culture is idealist, since he sees the artifacts of the human past as objects transformable by their readers into living thought and the aggregate of cultural artifacts as transformable into a collective mind ("that great poem which all poets, like the co-operating thoughts of one great mind, have built up since the beginning of the world"). On the other hand, the possible excesses of this idealist position are partly offset by his Empirical awareness that cultural artifacts attain life only by being transformed in the perception of living persons, who by their readings not only bring the past alive but also transform it in the process of formulating changed human circumstances. This Empirical awareness leads him to an appreciation of the frailty of culture, which constantly must live or die in the responses of the living. Like the Shelleyan poem itself, Shelleyan culture can continue to exist only through incessant transformations. This is a noble conception, and yet it also is clearly perilous. Shelley's high hopes for culture anticipate the Victorian humanist view of culture as a heaven and of art as a substitute for religion.[5] We have not been able to sustain that kind of optimism; few of our contemporaries would want to say with Shelley that "Poets are the unacknowledged legislators of the world," and probably few poets would want to take the burden of such a role upon themselves. Our skepticism has become far more radical than Shelley's.

But if Shelley's faith in culture today seems rather excessive, his defense of poetry as a valid mode of knowledge remains extremely powerful. If one allows his fundamental assumption, that ontology is impossible—that we can know truths, but never Truth—then poetry emerges as a significant method of formulating a certain class of truth. For him, poetry becomes the making of a world out of ourselves, which allows us to know ourselves in a way not otherwise possible. In the creation or reading of poetry we find that insight emerges from contexts, and the process of discovering truth becomes tantamount to the process of successfully formulating global contexts. Truly, the poem is a world; but just as truly, an indefinite number of poems can be formulated, which points toward an indefinite number of human worlds. Poetry becomes the mode of human freedom as well as of knowledge—and here, perhaps, Shelley also exhibits his limitations since he clearly preferred idealist worlds and found it difficult to perceive the context of human culture with the tolerance and breadth that we might wish for. But this does not invalidate his powerful insight that in poetry man makes himself by transforming himself into a world, and must continually create in order to continue his existence. As Wallace Stevens expresses it in *Notes Toward a Supreme Fiction*:

> There was a will to change, a necessitous
> And present way, a presentation, a kind
> Of volatile world, too constant to be denied,
>
> The eye of a vagabond in metaphor
> That catches our own. The casual is not
> Enough. The freshness of transformation is
>
> The freshness of a world. It is our own,
> It is ourselves, the freshness of ourselves,
> And that necessity and that presentation
>
> Are rubbings of a glass in which we peer.

NOTES

1. F. R. Leavis, "Shelley," in *Revaluation: Tradition and Development in English Poetry* (New York, 1947), pp. 203–40.

2. T. S. Eliot, "Shelley and Keats," in *The Use of Poetry and the Use of Criticism: Studies in the Relation of Criticism to Poetry in England* (London, 1933), pp. 87–102.

3. Matthew Arnold, *Essays in Criticism, Second Series* (1888). This phrase is coined in "Byron" and repeated in "Shelley." Actually, it was Hazlitt who first made this case powerfully. From "On Paradox and Commonplace," *Table Talk* (1821–22): "His bending, flexible form appears to take no strong hold of things, does not grapple with the world about him, but slides from it like a river." Quoted in Newman Ivey White, *The Unextinguished Hearth: Shelley and His Contemporary Critics* (Durham, N.C., 1938), p. 270. Also, from an unsigned review of *Posthumous Poems* in the *Edinburgh Review* (July 1824): "Mr. Shelley's style is to poetry what astrology is to natural science—a passionate dream, a straining after impossibilities, a record of fond conjectures, a confused embodying of vague abstractions—a fever of the soul, thirsting and craving after what it cannot have, indulging its love of power and novelty at the expense of truth and nature, associating ideas by contraries, wasting great powers by their application to unattainable objects. Poetry, we grant, creates a world of its own; but it creates it out of existing materials. Mr. Shelley is the maker of his own poetry—out of nothing." Quoted in *Shelley: Shorter Poems and Lyrics: A Casebook*, ed. Patrick Swinden (London and Basingstoke, 1976), pp. 54–55.

4. For an account of how modern poetry has tried to rest in the object, see J. Hillis Miller, *Poets of Reality: Six Twentieth-Century Writers* (Cambridge, 1965), and especially chapter I, "The Poetry of Reality."

5. The difficulties with that Victorian view are well demonstrated in the criticism of Matthew Arnold. For an account of Arnold's work, see J. Hillis Miller, "Matthew Arnold," in *The Disappearance of God: Five Nineteenth-Century Writers* (Cambridge, 1963), pp. 212–69. "Arnold's notebooks and his social, literary, and religious criticism . . . reject the present and embalm a dead vision. For 'the best that has been thought and said in the world' is no longer current in society. It is kept alive, in these bad times, only by the effort of the critic to 'learn and propagate' it, as a corpse might be kept alive by mesmerism. . . . Arnold the critic can only say: 'God exists, and I know it, but I do not know it directly, and I know too that He would be the only support of a civilization built on eternal values. Unfortunately, at this particular moment I cannot tell you, and no man can tell you, what those values are'" (pp. 263–64).

Index